Unleashing the Power of Perceptual Change

THE POTENTIAL OF BRAIN-BASED TEACHING

Renate Nummela Caine and Geoffrey Caine

Association for Supervision and Curriculum Development
Alexandria, Virginia USA

Association for Supervision and Curriculum Development
1250 N. Pitt Street • Alexandria, Virginia 22314-1453 USA
Telephone: 1-800-933-2723 or 703-549-9110 • Fax: 703-299-8631
Web site: http://www.ascd.org • E-mail: member@ascd.org

Gene R. Carter, *Executive Director*
Michelle Terry, *Assistant Executive Director, Program Development*
Ronald S. Brandt, *Assistant Executive Director*
Nancy Modrak, *Director, Publishing*
John O'Neil, *Acquisitions Editor*
Julie Houtz, *Managing Editor of Books*
Margaret Oosterman, *Associate Editor*
Gary Bloom, *Manager, Design, Editorial, and Production Services*
Karen Monaco, *Senior Designer*
Tracey A. Smith, *Production Manager*
Dina Murray, *Production Assistant*
Valerie Sprague, *Desktop Publisher*
Sarah Allen Smith, *Indexer*

Printed in the United States of America.

ASCD Stock No.: 197170
ASCD member price: $15.95   nonmember price: $18.95   s11/97

Library of Congress Cataloging-in-Publication Data
Caine, Renate Nummela.
   Unleashing the power of perceptual change : the potential of brain
-based teaching / Renate Nummela Caine and Geoffrey Caine.
      p. cm.
   Includes bibliographical references and index.
   ISBN 0-87120-287-5 (pbk.) : $18.95
   1. Learning, Psychology of. 2. Teaching—Psychological aspects.
3. Brain. I. Caine, Geoffrey. II. Title.
LB1057.C34 1997
370.15'23—dc21   97-33743
                                                  CIP

01 00 99 98 97   5 4 3 2 1

Unleashing the Power of Perceptual Change: The Potential of Brain-Based Teaching

WITHDRAWN

Preface

Together with our friend and colleague Sam Crowell, we plunged in to coach two schools in what we then called brain-based learning. Our experiences with these schools and countless others followed the publication of *Making Connections: Teaching and the Human Brain* by ASCD in 1991. To say that what we learned could fill volumes is no exaggeration.

Originally, we had negotiated with ASCD to write one book documenting our experiences and our learning. Cutting our writing to the bare bones, we were nevertheless unable to reduce the manuscript below 400 pages. Editors and writers alike decided that the book was too long and coverage too vast. We decided instead to create two books and, in the process, do justice to what we were trying to say. The result was *Education on the Edge of Possibility*, and now, *Unleashing the Power of Perceptual Change: The Potential of Brain-Based Teaching*.

We have often spoken with colleagues in the neurosciences, biology, and computer technology about how their work can help schools. Frequently, they have expressed bitter discouragement at the seemingly immense barriers provided by systemic and often unquestioned procedures and processes that enmesh the typical school. These barriers have seemed impenetrable to them. Innovative educators, of course, have had similar experiences. With all the research available on learning and teaching, with all the voices over the years—from Dewey to Combs, to Sarason to Goodlad (to mention a few)—all spelling out how schools need to change, we haven't been able to genuinely say that much progress has been made.

In *Education on the Edge of Possibility,* we look at the systemic features that keep our old model in place. We paint a picture of the tide that is carrying all of us into a new world. We suggest that we are all on a large ship that has already left port.

We now suggest that the notion of one ship is inappropriate, and that to traverse the turbulent waters on which we find ourselves, a fleet of ships may be a more appropriate metaphor. Whether it's charter schools or home schooling, distance education or corporate schools, or some other creative configuration, technology and other forces will make these new versions of schooling attractive and cost-effective.

Our experiences with schools and teachers have also convinced us that these physical reconfigurations will not be enough. To extend the metaphor, the ships may be redesigned, but most of them are still being sailed in the same old way. We desperately need to change our collective thinking and to take advantage of the research in learning, including the neurosciences. Understanding how humans learn needs to become the cornerstone for understanding how to teach. Additionally, we suggest that we educators take a completely new look at human potential and our ability and need to learn throughout life.

Somewhere in our notes, we wrote down, "When will we ever stop looking at why things don't work and begin to become excited about possible solutions?" Ultimately, both books are meant to shed some light on genuine change and give a glimpse of the many options open to us as educators. Such change will take a great deal of courage, and belief in ourselves and in a universe filled with promise instead of danger.

In this book, we unveil the different perceptual realities, or perceptual orientations, that seem to us to frame the ways in which people think about education and teaching. We then illustrate the different instructional approaches that we identified. Finally, we spell out why we believe that the future demands an education grounded in what we call Perceptual Orientation 3, with its view of a dynamic and interconnected universe, and why teachers at Perceptual Orientation 3 need to be proficient in all three instructional approaches. More specifically, we suggest that brain-based teachers are those who function at the Perceptual Orientation 3 level and who also share our theory of learning and of practice, grounded in its link with the neurosciences.

We have many people to thank. First are those educators with whom we have worked and shared, and from whom we have learned so much. In the schools where we worked in depth, several people trusted us, took risks beyond the call of duty, and helped us with this book. They include Sharon Bannister, Cathy Berry, Ellen Giffen, Sharon Smith, Carol Lawrence, Doris Lombard, Gareth Montgomery, Donna Orr, and Randy Peters. We are deeply indebted to the administrators who worked with us, specifically Kris Halverson, Cindy Tucker, and Melissa Proffitt. Special thanks go to the Illinois Academy of Math and Science, a superb high school and one whose teachers we quote at length in this book. They include Michael Dehaven, Sue Eddins, Chuck Hamberg, Bernie Hollister, Elia Lopez, Ed Moyer, Christian Nokkentued, Martha Regalis, and David Workman. Similarly, we thank members of Project Learn (LAMP) in Los Angeles; their responses were among the most helpful in clarifying our thinking. Thanks are also due to all those individuals who participated in our research across the United States, the various teacher education programs and universities, and especially Linda Little Ellis, whose dissertation lent much support and confirmation to what we were observing in teacher change.

Throughout our writing, we have had rewarding conversations with and been inspired by many individuals. They include John Abbott, Art Combs, Dee Dickinson, Sally Goerner, Myron Kellner-Rogers, Stephanie Pace Marshall, and Meg Wheatley. A special note of thanks goes to our dear friend Duncan Johnson. We should add that Judy Haney has been invaluable in assisting us with the transcription of many interviews and the preparation of the manuscript and bibliography. We continue to be indebted to Lynn Nadel at the University of Arizona. And we really appreciate the work and patience of our editor, Margaret Oosterman.

Finally, and most important, we would like to express our gratitude to ASCD Assistant Executive Director Ron Brandt for his vision. When it comes to education, he has perhaps the broadest "cognitive horizons" of any editor. It took his genius to invite the possibilities.

1

The Clash of Two Worlds

Why is the educational world in such turbulence? How is it possible that some states are just waking up to the "magic" of whole language, while others have made the word an unmentionable? Why is outcome-based education under fire, while phonics is celebrated as a new solution to literacy? Why are vouchers lauded as the new solution to restoring education to its past excellence? What is behind all these often passionate and frustrating arguments?

As educators, we are often reminded of the "Push me-Pull you," the animal in Dr. Dolittle that has a head at each end. Thus, it faces in two directions at one time. Education today is often like that creature: One piece is moving forward, another wants to go back, and the middle feels the tension. That tension is the key to our appreciation of new possibilities, because, like so many other social systems today, education is on the edge of possibility.

What Does Living on the Edge of Possibility Mean?

We believe society is in the throes of phenomenal changes—driven by changing definitions of science, the continuous expansion of

1

technology, research in the neurosciences, globalization of markets and cultures, and other factors. We are only beginning to explore how these discoveries affect our understanding of organizations and our collective beliefs about learning and schooling.

In part, the edge of possibility refers to the almost out-of-control explosion in knowledge and technology where possibilities are continually explored. Such explorations range from developing sophisticated learning software to applying nanotechnology. The opportunities and implications for our collective futures appear endless. In part, living on the edge of possibility is personal: It requires individuals to be comfortable with uncertainty and change. And, in part, the edge of possibility has a more technical meaning: It refers to the state of a system (sometimes called the edge of chaos) where dynamical change takes place in a way that ultimately sustains life and the system itself.

Why Is Living on the Edge of Possibility Important to Educators?

Even though our generation may find that adapting to this emerging world—where continuous change rules—is difficult, our students are inheriting it as a way of life. Society needs educational systems that are designed for a world of possibilities and teachers who can help students survive and master that world.

We started our journey into schools five years ago, when we began to implement and further research the ideas we had developed in *Making Connections: Teaching and the Human Brain* (Caine and Caine 1994a). We sought to develop what we called brain-based teachers, and we thought we knew what that phrase meant. Over time, we began to see that what we called brain-based teachers meant teachers who were at home on the edge of possibility. Even more important, as we researched what made these teachers different, we began to see patterns of beliefs and perceptions that are driving educational change. Like the "Push me-Pull you," some of us in education are ready to experiment with possibilities; others are searching for certainty. We speak different languages and experience different realities.

This book documents our voyage of understanding, as we watched a number of teachers change from individuals who use traditional teaching and beliefs about learning to those who are at home in messy, rich, complex environments where possibility and opportunity rule. We found a richer appreciation of the complex relationship between education and the larger society that it serves.

The Coevolution of Education and Society

In *Education on the Edge of Possibility* (Caine and Caine 1997), we explore how the education system of the last 100 years has been a superb match for the Industrial Era (provided that we ignore many issues of social justice). In effect, the economy and education co-evolved. As factories developed and the nature of work changed in the latter part of the 19th century, society demanded that large numbers of people be educated to satisfy the needs of industry. Mass education for identifiable skills was required. A factory assembly-line model for schools made sense in this context. The management model that permeated industry—the model of hierarchies and bureaucracies—also made sense for the administration of education. In addition, the mode of instruction, whereby those with the information organized it and delivered it to students who needed to absorb it, was also a natural fit.

When viewing the system as a whole, that many people fell through the cracks did not seem to matter. Such disregard was in part based on the belief that many who did not receive a "good" education could nevertheless find work or operate businesses. Indeed, many of the most successful and wealthy people in the last century had a limited education. Even the university model that evolved was an appropriate adaptation, matching Industrial Era thinking. A select number of students entered higher education and went on to develop and refine the knowledge base of society as a whole.

Learning came to mean absorbing fragmented and categorized pieces of information. Students were evaluated on how much of this information they absorbed, and they were considered educated if they could prove that they had the basic concepts and skills needed to work in more or less predictable jobs they would have for a lifetime. The Industrial Era model for schools can be spelled out in the following way:

Only experts create knowledge.
Teachers deliver knowledge in the form of information.
Children are graded on how much of the information they have stored.

This model achieved great success. Even today, such an approach to education is emulated around the world. The obvious question is, why do we have to change?

The Industrial Era was marked by a type of stability based largely on beliefs about the world and our place in it. At its heart is a mechanistic worldview grounded in ideas from Sir Isaac Newton. Collectively, we believed in linear, systematic, cause-effect relationships. We assumed that inputs and outputs could be reliably measured and quantified independent of many aspects of a broader more elusive context. The industrial and Newtonian perspective led us to believe that when we take things apart, study smaller and smaller fragments, and search for answers in a measured fashion, we would find how everything fits together. And, of course, this belief was true in many contexts. Assembly lines and the flight of the space shuttle are two examples. We also applied the same thinking to social systems, including schools. Indeed, we could call schools and other bureaucratic modes of organization social machines (see Caine and Caine 1997).

In recent times, people's grasp of how social and other systems work has undergone a profound shift. Buffeted by research in the neurosciences, the reshaping of science itself, and massive and continuous shifts in technology, society has needed to change metaphors, from assembly lines to living systems. Living systems are not linear. They have patterns of change that appear unpredictable because they are interconnected with their immediate environment. They are in relationship to each other, and they thrive on information. They act lawfully, but the laws they abide by appear "messy."

The ideas about living systems are far more complex than the mechanistic ideas that have guided us in the past. Some are finding their way into the schools in the form of more fluid notions of intelligence, whole language, cooperative learning, and experiential education. Such approaches pay attention to the context as well as to the content. And both context and content are based on new approaches to how learning itself actually happens. This shift is profound.

To those who have invested in the industrial model of education, these new approaches to teaching are unfamiliar and may even seem invasive, given the old, linear view of learning. The approaches remain poorly understood by the public at large and by educators themselves. Although a rich research base backs many programs, their implementation in schools and classrooms is often inconsistent and shows widely varying results.

We contend in this book that, collectively, we have to understand that education in the Information Age will be profoundly different from education for the Industrial Era. We have to understand that schools and teaching are going through a shift that not only engages practice but also affects fundamental beliefs in what teaching is meant to accomplish, how it is done, who our learner is, and what is possible for the average human being to achieve.

Core developments are generating new possibilities and forcing all of us to face our traditional beliefs. In Figure 1.1 (see p. 6), we show the major transitions through which education and society have progressed as they coevolved. The model of education that served agrarian society was based on apprenticeships. People learned from partially directed experiences in families and groups within which they lived. With the shift to the Industrial Era, the factory model of education emerged, which we describe in this chapter.

Our society is now well into the Information Age, and education has no choice but to follow suit. The challenge is to participate intelligently in the change. To meet the challenge, educators must have a state-of-the-art understanding of how the brain functions and people learn. Education needs to be extremely well grounded in what is possible for humans to participate more fully in what they and society ultimately become. Thus, we begin with some emerging understandings about the brain and education.

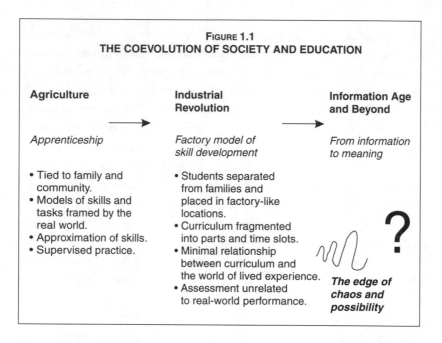

FIGURE 1.1
THE COEVOLUTION OF SOCIETY AND EDUCATION

Agriculture	**Industrial Revolution**	**Information Age and Beyond**
Apprenticeship	*Factory model of skill development*	*From information to meaning*
• Tied to family and community. • Models of skills and tasks framed by the real world. • Approximation of skills. • Supervised practice.	• Students separated from families and placed in factory-like locations. • Curriculum fragmented into parts and time slots. • Minimal relationship between curriculum and the world of lived experience. • Assessment unrelated to real-world performance.	**?** *The edge of chaos and possibility*

Brain Research

We live in an age where the biological sciences are peering deeply into how our brains work. Although brain research is often so narrowly focused that it appears to have little to offer educators, when findings of neuroscientists are matched with findings in other domains, the implications are breathtaking. Collective, often overlapping research is showing that most of us are born with vast and generally unused capacities—capacities that make even the most complex computers look simple in comparison.

Everything Is Connected

Perhaps most important is the growing evidence that our brains are whole and interconnected. Even though there are a multitude of specific modules with specific functions, thought and emotions, physical health, the nature of our interactions with others, even the time and environment in which we learn, are not separated in the brain. They are not dealt with one thing at a time. A whole event is registered and colors or influences how and what we learn. Areas of the brain interact like an interdependent web. At the heart of that web is the "I" that each of us knows as "me." The brain does not distinguish between school and real life. People and schools have created that distinction, but from the perspective of the brain, that distinction is purely artificial. Understanding this interconnectedness is critical:

> When I say that body and brain form an indissociable organism, I am not exaggerating. In fact, I am oversimplifying. Consider that the brain receives signals not only from the body but, in some of its sectors, from parts of itself that receive signals from the body! The organism constituted by the brain-body partnership interacts with the environment as an ensemble, the interaction being of neither the body or the brain alone. But complex organisms such as ours do more than just interact, more than merely generate the spontaneous or reactive external responses known collectively as behavior. They also generate internal responses, some of which constitute images (visual, auditory, somatosensory, and so on), which I postulate as the basis for mind (Damasio 1994, p. 88).

Learning theorists experimenting with this notion are beginning to show how interconnected a learner's brain is. For example, in one instance, theorists demonstrated that when children participated in a choir for only six weeks (exposing them to music and singing), the children's ability for spatial reasoning was significantly increased (Martin 1994). Spatial reasoning is engaged in all types of interior design and in space craft maneuvering. Music and mathematics are also known to be intimately connected, and learning to read affects one's ability to do abstract reasoning. Abstract reasoning is the basis for scientific inquiry and logical thinking. In the learner's brain, everything builds on everything else.

We Are Innately Motivated to Search for Meaning and Make Sense of Experience

Unlike a computer, human learning involves questions such as, Do I want to learn this? Have I ever wondered about that? Is this related to

7

what I already know? How does this make sense? What do I get when I learn this? Do the people I love and respect do this?

Although these questions are rarely asked consciously, they represent the gateway to learning anything significant. Learning is hard when devoid of reason or purpose—when there is no link to our personal needs. Indeed, by acknowledging and respecting student purposes, educators can teach to expand dynamical knowledge rather than simply to force-feed facts to be memorized. Most of us can remember being forced to learn something we hated. Few of us can say that we still use what we were forced to learn, unless such learning ultimately became a part of our greater life interest or purpose.

In effect, emotion and thought shape each other and cannot be separated. Emotions and feeling color meaning and value and are the energizers of attention and memory.

The Physiology of the Brain Is Changed by Experience

In addition to changes in behavior and perception, learning has a physiological component. The brain itself is physically altered by experiences, a phenomenon called plasticity. Plasticity refers to the change and growth in synaptic connections (connections between neurons); it also refers to changes in the strength of the synaptic connections and other factors even less understood. Thus, a new theory about volume transmission, for example, suggests that electrical waves sweep through the extracellular space in the brain in ways that may also have an impact on our understanding of learning (Agnati, Bjelke, and Fute 1992).

In the early years, from birth to age 3, brain and synaptic growth occurs through leaps and bounds, not one step at a time. For example, a mother's smile and daddy's attention result in physiological changes in an infant's brain, including neuronal branching (development of neuronal networks), which are then ready to add new branches. Peter Huttenlocher, a scientist at the University of Chicago, has documented and counted the number of neuronal connections by "measuring" these infinitesimal connections in individuals of varying ages:

From autopsies of the brains of fetuses and people ranging in age from a few months to their nineties, he took samples about the size of the head of a pin, each containing about 70,000 brain cells. In a sample from a 28-week-old fetus, he found 124 million connections between the cells. The same-size sample in a new-born had 353 million synaptic connections, and in an 8-month-old, the number exploded to 572 million (Kotulak 1996, p. 6).

Moreover, research now shows that many of the body's and brain's main systems develop concurrently. To the young child, every event embodies information that links to current, past, and future learning.

Although the brain is far more plastic in the early years, plasticity continues for life. Neuroscientists, however, disagree about how much learning in later years involves the formation of new synaptic connections, as distinct from simply strengthening connections that were established early in life.

Implications for the Young Learner

Although every infant comes into the world with a genetic blueprint, how that blueprint is expressed depends on the child's interaction with her environment. That interaction builds a brain with its own unique design, features, and capacities. The infant is born with more brain cells and possible connections than will ever be needed. One reason appears to be that nature wants to assure the survival of this individual. Another reason is that the child is born ready to translate experiences into physical architecture, and the brain comes prepared to make this process happen. The overabundant brain cells take on roles as needed by the growing brain and the experiences that it has (Kotulak 1996).

The brain is a supersponge from birth to approximately age 3 or 4. Research shows, for instance, that at birth, an infant can master the sounds of any language. By 6 months, some of that capacity is reduced, and by 1 year, the child's primary accent has already begun to be shaped (Kuhl 1994). This phenomenon has been described as developing the perceptual representations of the sensorimotor basis of a language. We are shaped by our culture in the early years, and it is then that the brain has the greatest capacity to organize itself and take advantage of its abundance of neurons to become grounded in language, music, math, and art. When opportunities are not provided and cells are not engaged, multitudes of possible connections are never made. Future learning is always still possible but more cumbersome.

A word of caution is due. The brain's capacity to learn so exuberantly is NOT a justification for force-feeding young children with drills and rote memorization. The young brain learns best from the way that it is engaged in social, emotional, and sensory experiences. What shapes the brain is the type of experiences that it has, not only the type of information that is packaged and presented to it.

Plasticity means that the brain records all events, not just positive ones. Particularly in infants and children, negative experiences associated with violence, hunger, and trauma can be "hard-wired." Thus, patterns of future dysfunction can become entrenched early in life. Generally, a good blueprint for health in the early years, when the brain is easily swayed one way or another, is to combine appropriate stimulation with a low-threat environment. The emotional climate is critical—safety in the form of a predictable world surrounding the infant, along with opportunities for all types of complex interactions. Such interactions include both physical and social contact with loving, responsible adults, together with a great deal of play and freedom to explore within safe parameters. Laughter, joy, love, and a relatively reliable schedule for everything, from changing diapers to nap time, become important because they spell a type of safety.

The opposite is a blueprint for disaster. Anything related to abandonment, from a largely unpredictable schedule for feeding to being moved from one strange caretaker to another in an unpredictable manner, can disrupt an infant's trust and increase the stress hormone level in the body. Large doses of stress hormones have been shown to inhibit new learning (Caine and Caine 1994a).

Even within these early years, critical periods seem to occur. These are optimal times for the development of some systems. Examples include some physical functions, such as vision and hearing. Critical periods for the development of many other skills and abilities also seem to occur, although these periods are not as explicit. They are the most beneficial times to introduce such skills and abilities.

The practical conclusion is that the early years are the bedrock for later success in almost every aspect of development, and that optimal ways for engaging the young learner exist.

Implications for the Early School Years

Although the brain continues to be a sponge until the preteens, the early school years matter more than we ever imagined. This is the time to learn languages, paint, create stories, and learn to play an instrument. It is the time to learn to read, work with mathematical puzzles, and investigate science and nature. These years should get the most attention—they are when the foundation for a healthy, intelligent, and talented adult is laid down. But along with more funding, fewer students in classes, and the best minds teaching our children, we need teachers and educators who understand how whole and interconnected learning really is. And they need to know how to teach children, given our new understandings of how learning happens.

If children are literally formed by their experiences, not just by memorization, then a teacher who knows how to fascinate students into wanting to write, read, play music, and discover the physical world can create miracles. It's not about teaching to kids. It's about creating hearty (socially and emotionally healthy), exciting, and fascinating experiences that invite learners to work hard while exploring how to do the things that challenge and intrigue them.

An example is the Suzuki method of teaching children to play the violin. Children listen to both beautiful music and favorite tunes, such as "Twinkle Twinkle Little Star." They listen alone and with their parents. They first learn to love the music they will learn to play, a phase we call getting a felt meaning. Then one parent begins taking lessons to play the instrument that the child will later adopt. Several months later, the child is introduced to that instrument and explores it with a parent naturally, both learning at the same time. Opportunities are provided for miniperformances, so that the child can demonstrate progress and everyone can express appreciation. Adults do schedule times for the child to practice, but practice is seen as part of everyone's love for music, garnering critical parental attention and approval. This method is quite different from learning to play an instrument unconnected to love of music or parental attention and encouragement.

Good teaching in the early years is time-consuming because so many aspects of the child's life have to be considered. Given the importance of the early years and the complex nature of learning and teaching, we should devote the major part of our resources here. In a very real sense, "it takes a whole village to raise a child."

Yet a number of our priorities are misdirected. In many states, we pay relatively little attention to the early years, encouraging mothers to work while children are in minimal or ineffective child care. Then we build prisons where cost can outdistance that of postsecondary education, as happened in California. We give teachers few resources and limit their disciplinary instruction to largely surface knowledge. We restrict teacher training to traditional teaching, rather than linking practice to how children actually learn, and we look almost exclusively to test scores as indicators of success. Given what we know about brain development, our approach is folly.

What About Older Children and Adults?

We can always learn more. But once the brain has organized into powerful and basic patterns, what is to be learned has to take these patterns into account. Adding to our already established patterns is still relatively easy; but changing the basic patterns is difficult for most adults. We end up with what Ellen Langer (1989) calls "cognitive commitments."

Evidence shows that exercises like meditation, "focusing," and reflection help us discern and even override basic patterns. This type of work is also what therapy promises to help one do. Some people spend much time and money on undoing inappropriate learning from childhood. Others simply use what they have as best they can and accept the patterns or limitations that their early learning created. Such patterns can, however, inhibit personal development and fuller use of our capacities:

A self-organizing world is best understood by delving into its paradoxes. Life, free to create itself as it will, moves into particular forms, into defined patterns of being. Pathways and habits develop, and over time, they become boundaries, limiting the freedom of self-expression. Who we are becomes an expression of who we decided to be. Our choices become limited as we strive to be consistent with the person we already are. We reference a self to continue creating a self, and the reference controls us (Wheatley and Kellner-Rogers 1996, p. 48).

Although most hard-wiring of the brain is laid down in the early years, and the brain itself becomes less malleable and changeable, the capacities of older brains are still extraordinary and, to a large extent, untapped. The primary reason is that people have failed to appreciate how profoundly interconnected and powerful the brain is, and have therefore not been able to leverage the specific skills and capacities on which so much attention has been focused.

As the future unfolds, we see a path showing us how to move forward:

1. People need to help learners more fully capitalize on the potential embedded in their brains.

2. The way to tap this potential depends on grasping more fully the interconnectedness within each brain.

3. At the same time that people come to terms with this higher-order level of brain functioning, they need to appreciate that the interconnectedness in the brain is an aspect of the interconnectedness inherent in all social and physical phenomena.

4. Thus, we are seeking to tap the brain's potential to prepare people to live in a new reality.

2

The Changing Face of Reality

The critical shifts required to guarantee a healthy world for our children and our children's children will not be achieved by doing more of the same. "The world we have created is a product of our way of thinking," said Einstein. Nothing will change in the future without fundamentally new ways of thinking.

—Senge, in Jaworski 1996, p. 9

The interconnectedness we see in the brain is actually representative of what we are beginning to see in almost any physical or social phenomenon. Thus, we are beginning to recognize that the future belongs to those who can grasp the notion of interconnectedness, wholeness, and complexity. As we noted in *Education on the Edge of Possibility* (Caine and Caine 1997), the paradigm shift is real. In the past, we have viewed schools as factories and the brain as a machine. The time has now come to see that the brain itself is a more accurate metaphor for the world in which we live.

Our generation grew up with the belief that things come in pieces and that those pieces are independent of other pieces. So we studied the individual pieces with the most sophisticated machines and technology we could invent. Only slowly, over time, by studying the individual bits did we learn that all the bits are connected, forming a whole we cannot always see but that exists nevertheless.

Future survival is linked to learning. We have to move, however, from learning that is fragmented to learning that is inclusive and helps us understand interconnectedness and the relationship of elements to each other. This need for a change is reflected in a gathering of people across professions:

> NAMBE, N.M. A linguist, a scientist, a journalist, and an artist gathered at an idyllic adobe retreat house here recently to identify a critical issue facing humanity. They emerged to inform several dozen guests that most of the world's ills can be traced to problems with learning: "The solutions begin with the lifelong human capacity to enjoy and share the process of learning," the four said in a statement. "Learning must become a means to bridge social fragmentation. Finally, we need to take responsibility for the way we act on our learning" (Nesmith, *L.A. Times,* August 1, 1996, p. A5).

Our picture of reality is being challenged and shifted in almost every field and profession. These changes are happening while too many school bells still ring every 50 minutes and learning is largely limited to memorization of teacher- or textbook-generated knowledge.

The New Science

In physics, those who have penetrated beyond Newton's world into that of subatomic particles are writing the rules governing our picture of what is and is not real:

> What we took to be sharply bounded objects—particles of matter—have turned out to be interwoven, overlapping aspects of each other. Every thing and every event in the universe seems to be attached to an all-embracing, quivering web that interconnects it with every other thing and event. Nothing stands apart. The cosmos as now portrayed by relativity and quantum mechanics is less like a loose collection of jiggling billiard balls and more reminiscent of a single, giant universal field—an unbreakable unity which Alfred North Whitehead dubbed "the seamless coat of the universe" (Darling 1996, p. 137).

The quantum mechanical universe is more like a primordial soup. We can detect it by studying patterns and tendencies, but it never stands still for long.

What the new science is teaching us is that the essential interwovenness of everything extends beyond the quantum world. The universe is far less a place where precise measurement rules than we originally thought. We are beginning to understand that the universe is continually changing and totally interdependent. Everything affects something, and ultimately, everything else:

> Evolution as survival of the fittest has inhibited our observation of coevolution. . . . We are not independent agents fighting for ourselves against all others. There is no hostile world out there plotting our demise. There is no "out there" for anyone to occupy. We are utterly intertwined. Always we are working out conditions for life with others. We play an essential role in shaping each other's behavior. We select certain traits and behaviors. They respond to us. Their response changes us. We are linked together. We codetermine the conditions of one another's existence. . . .
>
> No one forges ahead independently, molding the world to his or her presence while the rest trail admiringly behind. We tinker ourselves into existence by unobserved interactions with the players who present themselves to us. Environment, enemies, allies—all are affected by our efforts as we are by theirs. The systems we create are chosen together. They are the result of dances, not wars (Wheatley and Kellner-Rogers 1996, p. 44).

We are all coinhabiting a web of existence in which every person, act, and event are interrelated in multiple and often invisible ways. Traditional notions of cause and effect are being questioned. We are becoming responsible for each other and for the planet.

Yet many of us persist in seeing actions, individuals, and events as relatively separate and isolated. Without an understanding of interconnectedness and complexity, we have a society that cannot understand or appreciate the implications of our instrumental "bits and pieces" approach to life. Insights derived from ecology can help us understand interconnectedness:

All members of an ecological community are interconnected in a vast and intricate *network* of relationships, the web of life. The members derive their essential properties and, in fact, their existence from their relationships to other things.

Interdependence is the nature of all ecological relationships. The success of the whole community depends on the success of its individual members, while the success of each member depends on the success of the community as a whole.

The stability of an ecosystem depends on the *complexity* of its network of relationships—in other words, on its *diversity*. In a diverse ecosystem, many species with overlapping ecological functions coexist and can partially replace one another (Capra, March 1995, p. 2)(emphasis in original).

The quote reminds us of something our 74-year-old neighbor said—when he was young, they believed that sewage thrown into the local river was gone because the river somehow cleaned itself. This is the same mentality that decided to sell PCBs and DDT to other countries when these substances were banned in the United States. Today, in contrast to our old paradigm of believing that things are independent of larger consequences and connections, we are discovering that chemicals we thought were safe are actually lethal when combined with other chemicals (Colborn, Dumanoski, and Peterson Myers 1996). We are genetically engineering plant and animal life for instrumental purposes, such as a longer shelf life, but understanding little about what this type of work will do to our world at more subtle levels.

The same holds true for medicines. They are studied to work for specific purposes, but few companies invest in research to find out how safe the medicines are when used in multiple combinations, or to find out how differences between individuals can influence the effect of the medicines.

Changes in Organizations and the Workplace

The notions of complexity and interconnectedness are also influencing how we look at organizations of the future. Companies are beginning to see that when we fragment people and departments, vital links between workers are lost—links that represent information that the entire organization needs to stay on top of the most current understandings and changes. When products become outdated, sometimes separate, bureaucratic procedures represent roadblocks and hazards. Even though bureaucracies were the ideal for the Industrial Era, they represent certain death for the company needing to live on the edge of possibility. A change requires a new understanding of how the whole functions together:

> Each of us has a brain that is a complex adaptive system in which neurons are the agents. Each of us has a mind that is a complex adaptive system in which symbols and images are the agents. When we come together as a group, we constitute a complex adaptive system in both a biological and a mental sense. It follows that all organizations are such systems. Organizations interact to form national economic, societal, and political systems, and national systems interact to form a global system, which interacts with natural systems to form an interconnected ecology. . . . All are complex adaptive systems, each one fitting into another (Stacey 1992).

The work world our students and children will enter will reflect these changes and our new understandings of interconnectedness. Here is a summary of some future work needs that we believe are realistic:

• Businesses will have global aspects, requiring individuals who are at home with diverse cultures, customs, and languages.

• In many jobs and professions, technology and education will separate the haves from the have-nots more so than in the past. There will be a critical need for people who can use computers creatively, not merely as a tool for enforcing bureaucratic rules within organizations.

• Companies will primarily be defined not only by their physical products but also by the talent of the individuals who make decisions. Efforts to assess the value of companies in terms of their human capital are going on now. Self-starters and self-motivated learners will be sought.

• Entrepreneurship will likely increase, and entrepreneurs will need more creativity and belief in themselves so that they can find unique services that provide for emerging needs.

• More workers will be self-employed or employed as consultants without company affiliation and benefits.

As a minimum, these are the sorts of capacities that schools need to be focusing on.

Schools are teaching students to prepare them for memorizing the parts in bureaucratically organized and controlled environments; schools are failing to produce self-motivated individuals who can think and live with complexity and ambiguity. The new view of organizations requires people who are profoundly creative and adaptable.

Technology

The control of information made the delivery method of instruction possible. The teacher, with the assistance of prescribed texts, had the information that students needed to acquire. The classroom walls effectively shut out other sources of input. And the bureaucratic model worked because it organized the stages in which information could be acquired. One major reason to change teaching is that schools are losing control of information.

Early evidence of this loss of control comes from the impact of TV. When students remember advertising jingles but not the facts of a subject, we know that something else is occupying their minds. Perhaps the single biggest breach in the wall of education has come from information technology. First, almost everything that can be found in a text can now be found on a computer. An example is new computers that come equipped with an entire encyclopedia. Second, information that is making textbooks and teacher knowledge obsolete is now online on the Internet and the World Wide Web and often is available for free. Third, societies' push to provide every student with a computer means that students can get this knowledge free. Fourth, much of what is online is inconsistent with what teachers say and with what many parents want their children to know and believe. The interactivity of technology means that students of almost every age can communicate with their peers and with others of different ages, both across nations and the planet.

The bottom line is that schools as the deliverers of essential information are slowly being bypassed. This process will continue, irrespective of how much a government legislates to preserve traditional modes of education. The flow of information can as little be stopped as a human being can stand on a beach and stop the tide.

Technology is perhaps the most visible aspect of interconnectedness. Using the Internet, virtual reality, interactive software, and over 500 TV stations, many students can already access information that surpasses textbook or teacher knowledge. So how will these students react to the careful and controlled dispensing of knowledge in bits and pieces, as they sit in rows unable to connect this information to the larger world and their own experiences? High school students already feel restless and hostile learning things that are relatively outdated, meaningless, and on someone else's time schedule. Technology, more than anything yet invented, is capable of profoundly changing our world and helping us utilize our brains to the fullest:

> Just as we are undoubtedly on the brink of new understandings about learning, so too are we on the brink of radical developments in technology, which are so fundamental that they hold the power to alter, not merely our education system, but also our work and culture. At its roots, however, this technological revolution puts learning and conventional education systems on a collision course. The traditional role of education has, for too long, been predominantly instructional and teacher moderated, but the essence of the coming integrated, universal, multimedia, digital network is discovery—the empowerment of the human mind to learn spontaneously, without coercion, both independently and collaboratively (Abbott 1995).

The Possible Human

Theorists have recently begun to drastically reconceive the notion of intelligence. For many years, the dominant notion was that the bulk of intelligence was fixed. This idea is the basis for much of the argument in *The Bell Curve* (Herrnstein and Murray 1994). Although a notion of this type may still be applicable in some areas, we now know that intelligence is much more complex than had been considered (Gardner 1993). The work of many experts contributes to this growth in understanding: Gardner (1993) (multiple intelligences); Sternberg (1988) (three intelligences, including an overarching executive intelligence); Perkins (1995) (reflective intelligence); and Goleman (1995) (emotional intelligence).

Even more important is the evidence that some types of intelligence are learnable. An example is reflective intelligence:

> [Reflective intelligence involves] coming to know your way around decision making, problem solving, learning with understanding, and other important kinds of thinking. . . . The stuff you get is very diverse—strategies, habits, beliefs, values, and more—but it's all part of knowing your way around (Perkins 1995, p. 236).

Reflection on one's own processes, what is generally called metacognition, and on parts of what we call active processing is the core of high-level learning, because reflection is how people extract meaning from experience. We now see that metacognitive capacities can themselves be further developed.

In *Education on the Edge of Possibility* (Caine and Caine 1997), we speculate about the types of capacities that a person in the future may need, capacities that we still identify collectively as intelligence. Our notion of intelligence has much in common with Maslow's (1968) notion of self-actualization:

> Here is our list of attributes that a more complex and integrated person might possess:
>
> • ***An inner appreciation of interconnectedness.*** In a world where everything is relationship, more is needed than to intellectually understand the concept of relationship. Rather, people need to have a "felt meaning" for the whole. . . . so that they naturally perceive interconnectedness rather than separation.

• *A strong identity and sense of being.* In a fluid and turbulent world, it is very easy to become confused and disoriented. People will need a coherent set of purposes, values, and beliefs. Moreover, those values should include an appreciation of life, opportunity, and respect for individual and cultural differences.

• *A sufficiently large vision and imagination to see how specifics relate to each other.* There is always more than we can know, and the extent of our ignorance is increasing. People will frequently, naturally, and inevitably come face to face with the unfamiliar, the unexpected, and the unknown. People will therefore need an internal frame of reference that enables them to make instantaneous connections, to relate the unknown to the known, to see patterns in the chaos, and to perceive commonalities. We call this capacity broader cognitive horizons.

• *The capacity to flow and deal with paradox and uncertainty.* We will all be living on the edge of possibility. It is a place of paradox, uncertainty, ambiguity, flux, emergence, and change. We need to have ways of thinking and interpreting that help us see pattern in paradox. Our modes of thinking will have to include and go beyond formal operations and formal logic. One type of thinking that is at home with paradox is creativity. Another is dialectical thinking, where "there is truth in all things but not one thing has all the truth," or where, in the words of Edward De Bono (1970), there is "yes," "no," and "po" (which induces other possibilities). At the same time, we will need to appreciate the constant mystery and to understand that at some levels, no fixed answers are possible. In essence, there will be a need for an understanding of process and the capacity to let go of many types of control.

• *A capacity to build community and live in relationship with others.* In a world where interconnectedness is fundamental and pervasive, we will need a new understanding of relationship, diversity, and community. Each person is deeply influenced by every other person. Thus, community becomes more than a caring group of people working and living together. Self-knowledge will be essential, as will authenticity and the ability to resolve conflict. All these skills will become more critical as we understand that our sense of self is partly defined by our sense of, and the nature of, our communities. Consequently, we will have to be able to function both as individuals and as parts of greater social wholes (Caine and Caine 1997, pp. 97–98) (emphasis in original).

We therefore argue that ethics and intelligence must be linked, because a person who appreciates the interconnectedness of all, acts accordingly; that is, caring for others is intrinsic to being whole and caring for self. We also suspect that the almost total distinction currently made between the individual and the community will have to be modified. In many respects, the brain is a social brain, and intelligence is a function of the way we interact in context. One probable result of grasping the notion of the interconnectedness of a social system is that an intelligent person will want to be a member of an intelligent—wide-awake—community.

Such a concept of the possible human seems difficult to accept today because of our obsession with identifying separate but common elements and ignoring interrelatedness. As we begin to appreciate the interpenetration of every skill, subject, and ability, we will be better able to grasp what relationship means.

We recall a segment in one of the original Star Trek TV shows, which exemplifies the distinction between current notions and the capacities of the possible human:

> The Klingons and the Federation are at war. Mr. Spock and Captain Kirk are trying to protect a planet of people who appear to refuse to recognize their predicament. Finally, when one or two of the inhabitants of the planet are killed, the Senior Council has had enough. It invites both parties to come to a meeting and as the officers enter, council members melt their weapons in mysterious ways. The council members simply suggest that they've had enough and that both the Federation and the Klingons will have to continue their disagreement somewhere else. It becomes obvious at this point that it was the council which held the cards all along. Members make one or more suggestions and then disappear in a burst of white light.
>
> In the final scene, Captain Kirk addresses Spock and says, "Report, Mr. Spock, what was that?"

Mr. Spock raises his famous eyebrows and replies, "I believe, Captain, we are to them as the amoeba is to us."

The task of educators is to assist students to function at levels higher than has ever before been sought on a wide scale. In the long term, education can no longer remain immune to the changes we have described.

The New Teacher

In *Education on the Edge of Possibility* (Caine and Caine 1997), we map out our sense of how systems function and how educators need to think about education in general. We also describe the approach that we use with schools, which we briefly summarize in the next chapter.

Given that society as a whole still needs education, and given that systems will function differently in the future, we began to see the need for a new picture of what it means to be a teacher in the 21st century. Teachers will need to be at home with a deep sense of complexity and uncertainty that allows them to "let go"and facilitate students to guide their own learning. What we didn't understand when we began was that for teachers to teach this way they had to transform their thinking.

More specifically, to engage in the complex modes of instruction that genuinely unleash student potential, an educator needs to have a particular outlook on reality. This outlook includes a fundamental appreciation for the interconnectedness of everything, including the different subjects of a curriculum and the relationship of curriculum to student life experiences. Ultimately, we discovered that the differences between teachers stem from profoundly different world views.

Our Purpose

In the course of four years, we implemented our approach to what we called brain-based learning—directly in two schools and indirectly in association with multiple schools, districts, and training institutions.

We observed and began to research different approaches to instruction, and we identified three sets of underlying beliefs and assumptions, what we call perceptual orientations.

We believe that most education is mired in Perceptual Orientation 1 thinking, which is at home with fragmentation of the curriculum, school day, and student mind. As we hope to show, Perceptual Orientation 3 educators are needed to unleash the power of human brains and to prepare people to function in a complex and extraordinary dynamical world.

This book describes our understanding of different approaches to instruction and our findings about the perceptual orientation that makes more complex instruction possible. We want to provide a means of communication that is desperately needed and sadly lacking. And we wish to support those who have embarked upon Instructional Approach 3 and share with them what we have learned in the hope that it will help them on their journey.

3

Implementing Our Theory of Brain-Based Learning

There's a moment in which some idea galvanizes all of us.
—Nesmith, *L.A. Times*, August 1, 1996, p. A5

Those who become comfortable with change and process, and with the ideas embedded in the new science, will frequently be at odds with those who rigorously hold on to the fundamentals of mechanism. The two groups will speak profoundly different languages and have different assumptions and meanings. Bridging these perceptual chasms will be one of the most crucial tasks for all of us in the coming years.
—Caine and Caine 1997, p. 77

Our initial reason for seeking change in schools was not sparked by public criticism of education or by the general momentum toward restructuring schools (although these helped propel our efforts). Our desire came first out of a respect for the research in learning, including findings from the neurosciences. We felt compelled to demonstrate that a more powerful approach to teaching and educating children would emerge if educators shifted their basic assumptions about learning.

The theory we developed was presented in *Making Connections: Teaching and the Human Brain* (Caine and Caine 1994a) and modified in *Education on the Edge of Possibility* (Caine and Caine 1997). In this chapter, we provide an overview of our key ideas and briefly refer to the process that brought these ideas into schools. We also introduce the instructional approaches and the perceptual orientations.

We began by working with two public schools, Dry Creek Elementary School in Rio Linda, California, and Park View Middle School in Yucaipa, California. At Dry Creek, we included the entire school in our five-year plan—principal, librarian, other nonteaching staff, and custodians. We saw every adult as a potential teacher because each came in contact with the students. At Park View, we worked predominately with one of four tracks, namely D-track.

Background: The Brain/Mind Learning Principles

Embarking on a change to brain-based learning and teaching begins with what we now call the brain/mind learning principles. Each principle represents an aspect of learning that summarizes multiple disciplines, including research from the neurosciences. The principles are based on research reported in formal journals and texts and are grounded in our experiences. These principles are not meant to represent the final word on learning. Collectively, they do, however, result in a fundamentally new, integrated view of the learning process and the learner. They move us away from seeing the learner as a blank slate and toward an appreciation of the fact that body, brain, and mind are a dynamic unity. They also challenge educators to go beyond a predominantly behavioral view of learning and teaching, which has dominated education for several decades.

We developed 12 principles (see Figure 3.1 on p. 28), which are described in other publications (Caine and Caine 1994a; Caine, Caine, and Crowell 1994; Caine and Caine 1997).

FIGURE 3.1
BRAIN/MIND LEARNING PRINCIPLES

Principle 1: The brain is a complex adaptive system.

Principle 2: The brain is a social brain.

Principle 3: The search for meaning is innate.

Principle 4: The search for meaning occurs through "patterning."

Principle 5: Emotions are critical to patterning.

Principle 6: Every brain simultaneously perceives and creates parts and wholes.

Principle 7: Learning involves both focused attention and peripheral perception.

Principle 8: Learning always involves conscious and unconscious processes.

Principle 9: We have at least two ways of organizing memory.

Principle 10: Learning is developmental.

Principle 11: Complex learning is enhanced by challenge and inhibited by threat.

Principle 12: Every brain is uniquely organized.

Source: Caine and Caine 1997, p. 19.

Introducing Our Change Process

The core of the process was the involvement of participants in what we call process groups, a study of the brain/mind learning principles, and reflection on their meaning. Participants used our workbook (*Mindshifts: A Brain-Based Process for Restructuring Schools and Renewing Education* [Caine, Caine, and Crowell 1994]), which focuses on a personal understanding of the principles. At both schools, we began with inservice sessions before placing everyone in process groups.

Although we initially established our own process for changing to brain-based learning, we found corroborating documentation for the change process in Routman's (1991) recommendations for teachers who are changing to a whole language approach:

1. Establish support groups that meet regularly. Put in place a three- to five-year staff development plan.

2. Allow voluntary attendance at support groups. Provide options in required staff development.

3. Read and discuss professional literature, attend conferences, and provide other opportunities for acquisition of theory.

4. Allocate adequate discretionary funds and make professional growth a priority. Have clear expectations for resourcing these opportunities.

5. Include teachers in curriculum design, district evaluation procedures, and hiring new teachers.

Our change process was a five-year plan. The process groups met weekly, and members explored their teaching in relation to the brain/mind principles. Moving toward an understanding of wholeness requires personal changes that cannot be forced or imposed from the outside; so working predominantly with volunteers turned out to be a critical factor. At Dry Creek, the entire school volunteered; at Park View, we also worked only with volunteers, with the most consistent participation (five years) coming from D-track.

During the first year, we focused on the brain/mind principles, with theory and instruction coming later. The entire change process included regular meetings (weekly for 1 to $1\frac{1}{2}$ hours at Park View; once a week for three weeks out of four at Dry Creek) and periodic inservice sessions that we conducted. We emphasized changing teacher beliefs in learning and teaching and helping teachers redesign their classrooms, school, and teaching as a result of their new understandings and group collaboration.

As change is thrust upon educators, and as much of their support dissipates, they find themselves in a catch-22. They are asked to take risks, be innovative, change, and improve education, but they have to make these efforts in a context that increases their downshifting (a psychophysiological response to threat associated with fatigue or perceived helplessness [Caine and Caine 1991, 1994a]). They must be innovative—and yet "get it right." Their students must perform at higher levels—and yet teachers have to apply a grading system that many think is nonsensical. Time lines that have little bearing on the task at hand but meet the needs of those higher up in the hierarchy are imposed on them. And they must work within the system as it has always been, which includes its dreams, wishes, envies, and politics.

We dealt with these concerns in the process groups. First, we addressed the power issue through group membership and the process. Membership was cross-functional and ideally reflected different layers of the hierarchy, so that a commonality of interest was created and people could meet each other as people, not just as representatives of the hierarchy. Second, we established periods of noncompetitive sharing, so that every person had absolute equality in terms of time and the importance of their contribution. Third, we insisted that every member have regular opportunities to act as both participant and facilitator, so that everyone could better appreciate the possibilities and responsibilities of being leaders and followers.

The result was that groups began to bond and establish a sense of community, a sense of safety, and a type of stability, which made dealing with the larger challenge easier. When combined, these conditions appeared to facilitate greater self-efficacy and authenticity, as teachers talked, experimented, became more honest about failures and successes, and began to acknowledge their own agency and individuality. Such changes have also been reported by Little (1982) and Goodlad (1984) among others.

As teachers in the two schools studied a brain/mind principle, we wanted them to understand that teaching to one domain, such as the affective domain, the cognitive domain, or the psychomotor domain, might make sense for research, but in a child's brain, all three domains and more are constantly interacting, supporting, and informing one another. Their question was inevitably, "What does such interaction mean?"

On the one hand, what they were learning was enormously liberating because it matched what they observed of their students in the classroom. On the other hand, how could one control something so complex? If emotion, cognition, and physical processes occur simultaneously, what are the implications for instruction? They began to realize that attention, as it is commonly described, is a complex process that becomes enhanced as more of the body, mind, and brain are engaged simultaneously. This understanding created further puzzles for teaching, and these had to be explored. Teachers were confronting their own beliefs about learning, which by implication resulted in examining what they were doing in the classroom and what the school and district were supporting.

The initial change process was slow, and we had to continually remind participants that they had permission to create and invent, using new understandings. We had to allow for their struggles and frustrations, even for their anger at what appeared to be our asking them to defy other authorities. Such feelings were particularly evident in the beginning, when it was hard for them to understand that our theory meant teaching content differently. They found moving away from rigidly interpreted guidelines (district or state) and using their own vision of learning to focus on the delivery of content to be difficult.

The Goal: Meaningful Learning

As a minimum, we wanted them to understand the distinction between a low-level yet pervasive knowledge outcome and one that is more demanding yet necessary if education is to function at higher levels. Thus, we argued that there is a difference between surface knowledge (rote-memorized facts and skills) plus technical or scholastic knowledge on the one hand and dynamical knowledge on the other.

Technical or scholastic knowledge refers to intellectual understanding. Such knowledge has a role in learning but is insufficient alone:

> It [technical or scholastic knowledge] is extremely important, irrespective of whether it is acquired in school or elsewhere; but it is limited because technical or scholastic knowledge, by itself, excludes what Gardner calls "generative" or "deep" or "genuine" understanding. That is, scholastic knowledge lacks a quality that

makes it available for solving real problems or for dealing with complex situations (Caine and Caine 1997, p. 111).

Dynamical knowledge connects to the real world of the student—it is knowledge that can be used naturally and spontaneously and demonstrated in authentic situations. It is through dynamical knowledge that transfer of learning becomes real.

We also introduced the idea of felt meaning. If cognition and emotion were interconnected, then real understanding would include an almost visceral sense of relationship with an idea, skill, or body of information. In more formal terms, underlying any deep understanding would be (borrowing from Pat Kuhl 1994) a "perceptual representation of a sensorimotor foundation." An example of felt meaning is an athlete who might work on the mechanics of how to pitch until everything "falls into place and just feels right." Felt meaning is also illustrated in a student who has a feel for math, a love of literature, or a gift for drawing. Teachers began to understand that teaching for genuine understanding and the feeling of meaning would be quite different from delivering information and asking students to memorize facts and procedures.

How to Teach for Meaning

We formalize our approach to instruction in *Making Connections* (Caine and Caine 1994a), where we suggest that all complex learning involves three interactive elements. These elements apply to all students, of all ages, and in all knowledge domains where genuine understanding and natural knowledge are desired:

- *An optimal state of mind that we call relaxed alertness, consisting of low threat and high challenge.*
- *The orchestrated immersion of the learner in multiple, complex, authentic experience.*
- *The regular, active processing of experience as the basis for the making of meaning.*

To help teachers understand these essential elements, we provided examples of experiences and ideas teachers could implement. But we thought that the school community should be responsible for choosing the actual instructional methodologies. Examples included materials published by the Lawrence Hall of Science, such as Math Renaissance, and Gardner's (1993) theory and related teaching practices compatible with the notion of multiple intelligences. Thematic instruction and cooperative learning were welcomed, as was whole language. We did not eliminate phonics or rote memorization; we simply asked teachers to understand the differences between the methods and tie them to student learning and our brain-based theory. We wanted their changes in beliefs and understanding of learning to drive their changes in instruction. We hoped to change and expand their mental models—the actual belief system that guided their moment-to-moment actions. We were trying to model our theory by asking teachers, nonteaching staff, and administrators to design what they were beginning to understand and apply their new understandings by making new choices. Figure 3.2 (see p. 34) shows the brain-based model we used.

Relaxed Alertness

Second, we suggested that an optimal state of mind exists for meaningful learning. We describe it as relaxed alertness, a combination of low threat and high challenge. This element should be monitored both in the entire school environment and in the classroom. Above all, we wanted staff and students alike to feel safe to take risks. The key was to ensure that a school became a coherent community. We explored orderliness and coherence, qualities that help children understand and feel that they are in a world that makes sense. Coherence is what results when complex adaptive systems reflect common purposes, meanings, and values.

Coherence involved simple decisions, such as how to organize into groups, how time works without bells, and how and when to perform certain responsibilities in the elementary grades. It also involved more complex components that tied into curriculum. For example, our approach to thematic instruction was to introduce a set of what we

Figure 3.2
BRAIN-BASED LEARNING MODEL

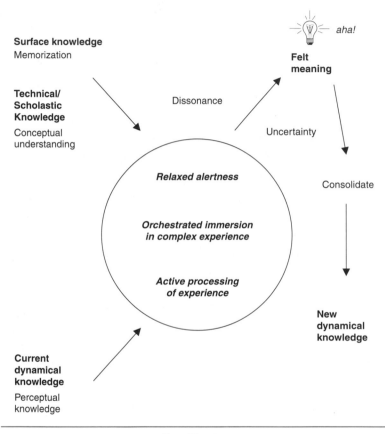

Surface knowledge
Memorization

**Technical/
Scholastic
Knowledge**

Conceptual
understanding

Dissonance

**Felt
meaning**

aha!

Uncertainty

Relaxed alertness

Consolidate

*Orchestrated immersion
in complex experience*

*Active processing
of experience*

**New
dynamical
knowledge**

**Current
dynamical
knowledge**

Perceptual
knowledge

Deep Meanings
Underlying purposes, values,
assumptions, and beliefs

Source: Caine and Caine 1997, p. 110.

called principles of connectedness, one of which is "order is present everywhere." This idea can be used to guide curriculum and instruction. It can also be used in staff meetings and on playgrounds. We wanted to show that in a truly coherent community, every aspect of functioning was interconnected.

Orchestrated Immersion in Complex Experience

The first element we explored together was immersion of learners in complex experience. We wanted teachers to move away from direct and text-driven teaching to explore meaningful and purposeful experiences with students. This element was clearly common to the young as well as to adults, and we wanted it to guide practice at every grade level. Those who caught on to what we were talking about began to introduce amazingly rich and complex worlds of experience into their classes. One of our favorites was a K–2 class that began to replicate the Amazon Jungle, illustrated by a vast paper tree that sprouted from the floor in the middle of the room and gradually took over walls and ceilings (confiscated, unfortunately, by the fire department).

Active Processing of Experience

We call the third element active processing of experience. Creating experiences for students in a low threat/high challenge environment is not enough. The knowledge and skills embedded in more complex and authentic types of environments must continually be consolidated. This consolidation naturally leads to ongoing assessment—students report on what they are doing, respond to teacher and student questions and comments, and demonstrate excellence.

Teachers support and encourage students primarily by challenging student thinking. They ask for hypotheses, making sure students identify their big ideas but also pay attention to details; question purposes; challenge conclusions; and model excellence by referring to other fields and disciplines, always with an eye to expanding student thinking.

Active processing has been the most challenging element to implement. Helping teachers understand that assessment doesn't just come at the end has proven enormously difficult. Active processing refers to the constant and ongoing intellectual challenge that comes from suggestions and questions during an experience. It includes a type of memorization we call creative rehearsal. At higher levels, it asks students to do metacognitive tasks, such as reflecting on an activity or their own contribution. It also requires students to think logically and utilize the scientific process. Active processing needs an environment that reflects an intelligent community where intellectual pursuits are seen as natural and interpersonal skills and responsibilities are continually honed.

Expected and Unexpected Results

Although we knew from the beginning that we would be recording and documenting our experiences, much of what we did in the way of quantifiable research emerged over time and was generated by our combined observations and questions. We began with the two schools by giving all involved adults the principles and theory and invited them to study and translate them into practice. We record in this book what happened as teachers, administrators, and others attempted to align their thinking and actions to the theory. We include our own puzzles, ultimate questions, and understandings, which eventually reached beyond the two schools to include others.

Our research included both systematic collection of data and naturalistic gathering of documented comments, discussions, impressions, and one-on-one conversations. Many unpredictable factors continually pressed themselves into our awareness and shaped our further thinking. Our approach simulated an hermeneutic spiral as we observed, discussed, and reflected on what we saw, questioned our premises, read profusely, and came back to the original questions. Once we found specific identifiable characteristics in a particular event, we developed appropriate tools to allow for systematically gathering data.

This process is how we corroborated the instructional approaches and the perceptual orientations.

The linchpin of our process was small-group meetings supplemented by occasional inservice sessions lasting one to four days. We also spent time with teachers individually. In these additional interactions, we dealt in more depth with practice and curriculum. Again, our goal was not to provide teachers with specific strategies but rather to engage them in thinking about the strategies and approaches that they were using. We offered suggestions and provided models, but we did not train them in specific methodologies.

As teachers discussed the brain/mind principles and linked their understandings to both their learning and teaching, small things began to change. They seemed to understand that low threat was something that should be embedded in the entire school, and that the peripheral environment mattered. Classrooms began to look warmer and more personal as teachers made changes that reflected a more homelike environment by adding items like tablecloths and plants. We heard classical music and saw classical and other art everywhere. Ceremonies were created and honored, and common schoolwide procedures were introduced. Teachers established linkages with parents, and our emphasis on the need for a supportive, orderly community was expanded.

In the course of this work, however, we became puzzled by some things we saw. Communities were bonding well, using our theory as a unifying element. We appeared to be working together toward common goals. But classroom observations revealed an enormous degree of inconsistency, not only in practice but also in understanding.

For many teachers, what we were doing simply did not fit into their deeply ingrained notions of how teaching should be done. Many were committed to implementing formal curriculum requirements, making sure students did what was asked (discipline), giving tests, and disseminating grades. And most of these activities were tied to specific time tables that the school or district mandated. We were asking them to change time-honored and district-mandated beliefs, and this change took enormous courage and a massive shift in assumptions.

At the same time, other teachers, using the same brain-based language, began to function in more sophisticated ways. They seemed to be more at home in "messy" and dynamic environments. They developed the ability to have children, even in K–2 classrooms, work in relatively self-directed small and large groups. Students became interested in more complex projects and ideas and revealed levels of understanding that the teachers had not expected. Clearly something both powerful and subtle was going on.

As we mention in *Education on the Edge of Possibility* (Caine and Caine 1997), we began to find significant differences in approaches to instruction, particularly in how the approaches dealt with complexity. We label the differences Instructional Approaches 1, 2, and 3. The differences between Instructional Approaches 1 and 3 were breathtaking. Instructional Approach 1 focuses on discipline as a means of getting students to learn, and the teacher manages instruction. Instructional Approach 2 focuses on tying technical and scholastic knowledge to critical concepts. Without this knowledge, active processing can become superficial and ineffective. Instructional Approach 3 teachers were so capable of making learning engaging and meaningful that discipline became a subsidiary and relatively unimportant concern. It became clear to us that Instructional Approach 3 was the one we were after.

As we dug deeper into these approaches, we found something unexpected—the differences were not simply a matter of different strategies or ideas about learning. A strong relationship appeared to exist between the three instructional approaches and three perceptual orientations we discovered.

The teachers we identified as Perceptual Orientation 1 thinkers were at one end of a continuum, and Perceptual Orientation 3 thinkers were at the other (see Figure 3.3 on p. 39). Perceptual Orientation 3 thinkers were capable of moving beyond bureaucratic, highly structured, and directed teaching to become at home with the kind of flow needed to challenge and engage student minds to the fullest.

Teachers could readily agree that learning should be interactive, but we kept observing a tight control over student explorations. For example, teachers determined what was to be studied by strictly following state guidelines and using study guides that publishers provided; decided how the subject would be studied; specified the evaluation method; and controlled the evaluation that was inevitably a grade. From our point of view, little interaction was apparent. From their point of view, because students were asked questions or students asked appropriate questions during designated times, they were participating in their own learning. Some teachers had groups with highly structured tasks—better—but a far cry from the freedom and self-organization we were looking for.

FIGURE 3.3
THE PERCEPTUAL ORIENTATIONS CONTINUUM

The Perceptual Orientation 1 End of the Continuum	The Perceptual Orientation 3 End of the Continuum
Reliance on the power of others.	Reliance on self-efficacy grounded in authenticity.
Reliance on a narrow prescribed teaching focus.	Reliance on one's own broad cognitive horizons.
Reliance on control as coercion.	Reliance on building relationships that facilitate self-organization.
Almost exclusive reliance on an external focus.	Reliance on an internalized sense of self-reference and process.

We began to examine the power of the perceptual orientations to keep learning predictable movement on the one hand and to facilitate movement toward possibilities on the other. This examination took us beyond brain research to look at the impact that the new sciences thinking has on our collective redefinition of reality. Such a search helped us put what we were seeing into a new perspective and understand why Perceptual Orientation 3 thinking is critical for systemic change. We also were able to define more precisely what we meant by a brain-based teacher.

Tensions in the System

Differences in the assumptions underlying the perceptual orientations explained much of the tensions we found in the larger system. In our view, a majority of schools and systems function at Perceptual Orientation 1. The type of complex instruction needed for the next century depends largely on Perceptual Orientation 2 and 3 thinking. The perceptual orientations represent world views so different that communication between individuals and institutions invested in a particular world view is often extremely difficult.

We found not only that many teachers had trouble moving toward a more complex, self-organizing model and thinking, but also that the system itself was not set up for this kind of thinking. For example, in creating learning communities of trust and communication in classrooms, teachers would work with students to decide collectively when to take a break. Students and teachers would then go off to their respective restrooms, remain in the class, or stand outside the classroom door and chat. Others observing such actions, who were still deeply organized by a controlled schedule, complained about what appeared to them as misbehavior or a lack of control. At the middle school, we were proud of the way our teachers were maintaining orderliness and coherence within their respective communities (no coercion, behavior modification, or posted rules); but others became extremely uncomfortable that students had so much freedom.

We see our work as previewing the future in education. It seems to us that several tendencies are competing. One is a back-to-basics movement that reflects Perceptual Orientation 1 thinking. Another is a reform movement grounded in satisfaction with the current paradigm, making it more sophisticated and pragmatic. That movement reflects Perceptual Orientation 2 thinking. And a third is a shift toward self-organization and self-directed learning, and grounded in a belief in interconnectedness. Such a shift represents Perceptual Orientation 3 thinking.

It is important to mention that at both schools, the mixture of perceptual orientations and instructional approaches often led to what we call the coattail effect. Teachers who merely observed or were innocently exposed to Instructional Approach 2 or 3 would alter their behavior. One example occurred when a teacher, conscious of developing community and its implication for a low threat/high challenge learning environment, greeted her students daily at the classroom door. The students loved it, and soon students from nearby classes greeted her, too. Another teacher started appearing at her own door to greet her students. On the surface, these activities could be interpreted as powerful change. And several at Park View have commented on the strong influence D-track has had on the rest of the school. We think that this type of secondary change may be positive in some sense, but that when teachers do not understand why they do what they do at significant enough depth, such changes tend to be superficial and last only until the interests go out of fashion. Understanding the purpose of teacher actions is critical and at the heart of understanding the perceptual orientations.

4

Approaches to Instruction

In *Education on the Edge of Possibility* (Caine and Caine 1997), we discuss the difference between espoused theories and mental models. Espoused theories are the formal explanations we give for our actions to frame what we do in a more sophisticated light. Mental models are theories-in-use, driving what we actually do. In other words, "human organization reflects cognitive organization" (Keidel 1995, p. 5). Espoused theories may not necessarily reflect our mental models.

Our Questions on Teacher Change

Even though we believed we were on the same wavelength as the teachers, we saw that some were not changing fundamental patterns. We began to examine what they were doing in relation to their mental model—that is, how their actions reflected deeper basic assumptions. We looked at what they actually did, ignoring their formal explanations, and found that observable, overall instructional patterns were playing out. These patterns influenced how teachers related to us and translated theory into action, and they organized how teachers implemented what we suggested.

Patterns of Difference: Approaches to Instruction

We believe mental models (theories-in-use) govern actions. Thus, the mental model a teacher holds about the teaching and learning process and actual instruction would reveal an observable pattern.

We began with a sense that different patterns existed and with the belief that our theory was sound. As we worked with and observed the teachers, we were able to identify behaviors that indicate what a teacher's mental model is and show when teachers have shifted out of time-honored patterns. We translated these clusters of behaviors into Instructional Approaches 1, 2, and 3.

We caution once more that these approaches are tendencies. In the language of complexity theory, they seem to represent "basins of attraction" (with corresponding field effects). Within each such basin, vast numbers of possible behaviors and individual actions, which can be interpreted in multiple ways, exist. We also caution that our work was a process of interpretation and inference from what people said and did, both spontaneously and after being questioned. There is much room for additional research. The overall propensities, however, help us understand what is happening and the radically different approaches to teacher change.

Indicators of the Instructional Approaches

We identified five significant indicators that show differences in instructional approaches (we suspect there are more):

- Objectives of instruction.
- Teacher use of time.
- Sources for curriculum and instruction.
- Teacher approach to discipline.
- Teacher approach to assessment.

It is important to understand that no single indicator determines an instructional approach. Rather, comprehensive and persistent behavior over time spells out a commitment to a particular approach.

In the rest of this chapter, we explain each instructional approach by describing the differences as we observed them in our five indicators. Next, we briefly profile how a teacher might demonstrate each approach and conclude with a commentary.

Instructional Approach 1

Instructional Approach 1 can be described as a stand-and-deliver model. The dominant influence on ideas about teaching seems to be linked to the teacher's past school experiences. The approach is compatible with a mechanistic and bureaucratic world view. In the last 50 years, it has also become synonymous with a behavioral approach.

Objectives of Instruction

• The teacher focuses on students' acquiring prespecified information, facts, and skills through memorization, practice, rehearsal, and repetition.

• From a brain-based learning perspective, the goal is students' acquiring surface knowledge.

• Applying the brain/mind principles, we see an emphasis on programming the taxon memory systems, which organize and store unrelated information.

Teacher Use of Time

To guide learning, the teacher imposes an artificial time schedule on students, not questioning the impact of a 50- to 55-minute period on instruction. Deadlines are based on how long something "should" take and do not include planning for student-articulated needs for time. In many lesson plans, the teacher specifies exactly how much time is to be spent on any given point and tends to become irritable if students request additional time.

Sources for Curriculum and Instruction

A designated curriculum guide, handbook, or other appropriate authorities spell out what students should learn. The teacher selects and presents the primary instructional sources: texts, manuals, lectures, and demonstration videos. Content is separated into designated subjects, which are themselves taught as a series of fragments and topics.

Teacher Approach to Discipline

Discipline refers to the procedures needed to govern behavior that disrupts instruction and teacher control. Authorities write the rules, which are covered in class and frequently posted throughout the school and in classrooms. The teacher specifies and periodically reviews all types of punishment and the behaviors that result in punishment. Behavioral approaches to discipline (e.g., "assertive discipline") are popular and considered helpful and appropriate.

Teacher Approach to Assessment

The basis for assessment is students' ability to replicate precisely what the teacher or instructional source has presented. Instruments usually include paper-pencil tests or quizzes, with true-false, multiple-choice, or right-wrong answers.

Instructional Approach 1 in Action

We illustrate Instructional Approach 1 by presenting two profiles. Profile 1 emphasizes how a teacher uses the stand-and-deliver model of teaching to control learning and student behavior. Profile 2 shows how using a prescriptive approach interferes with students' natural curiosity.

Profile 1: Following a Teacher-Controlled Model

Jenny is in her thirties. She is an experienced teacher, and her principal is pleased with her performance. She is well organized and rarely sends students with discipline problems to the counselor or other authority. If a student is referred, the counselor knows that the problem is genuine and not the result of a teacher who cannot control her class.

Jenny is comfortable with behavioral objectives. She knows what is to be taught and where she is going; the students trust her to lead them. Lesson plans, often from previous years, provide structure. Teaching is not difficult because she tends to split learning into manageable chunks that are learned one at a time. She also believes that breaking up instruction is the best way for children to learn the material.

Students are allowed to participate in learning, but Jenny interprets participation to mean tightly controlled activities she directs. Examples include her reading aloud, then selecting textbook questions to ask students. Student responses may include board work to make a change and seat work to correct what another student has done. While individual students are performing, Jenny expects the rest of the class to be quiet and observe. That they may be bored, and that this boredom is often legitimate because students are at different levels of expertise and interest, do not occur to her. She believes that students derive meaning from content that she, as the teacher, presents, and from the designed lesson plan—not from personal connections and purposes.

Quizzes, tests, and firm disciplinary procedures are the primary motivators to assure that learning occurs and to verify that each fragment is learned and understood. Students complete each task; the teacher records every quiz and test result. Grades are based on the accumulation of points or on percentages and made available to students, parents, and other authorities. Jenny understands the concept of the bell curve and grade inflation, which she uses as guides to ensure that proper grading perspectives are maintained.

Commentary on Profile 1

Many teachers share Jenny's beliefs about school and her approach to instruction. As we began working with schools, the vast majority of the teaching we observed was at Instructional Approach 1.

If we ask Jenny how she believes students learn, she may give us a formal explanation such as, "learning happens when students understand the meaning of information." She may, therefore, agree overtly with a constructivist view of learning, a brain-based view, or a whole language approach. As we observe Jenny actually teaching, however, we notice that her instructional approach focuses on memorizing concepts, topics, and skills. That type of learning was used in schools over 20 years ago. Her theory-in-use, or mental model, defines understanding as students' doing well on a test; meaning refers to students' demonstrating what the teacher is looking for.

We would therefore say that her mental model, the theory that actually guides her instruction—from planning to assessment—does not match the complexity of her espoused model, which requires a more sophisticated approach to instruction. Although she believes that she is promoting meaningful learning and understanding in class, she does not develop these concepts well.

Jenny's instructional approach determines what she sees. During our observations, what struck us again and again was the overriding tendency of Instructional Approach 1 teachers to reduce new ideas and procedures to the same type of teaching that they had always done. Even when they were exposed to the identical words, descriptors, and instructional help as everyone else, these teachers could not let go of their overriding emphasis on students' mastering information, and the fact that such mastery was almost exclusively tied to what the teacher did with, or expected of, the students.

What we found most profound was that higher-order thinking, genuine reflection, and connection to real-life experiences were lacking. Student-teacher exchanges were inevitably limited to lecture and direct questioning. Teachers primarily used strategies and procedures for memorization, accompanied by an extreme emphasis on correct behavior and discipline. In fact, this emphasis on teacher control and classroom discipline is perhaps the most directly observable and distinguishable indicator of a teacher or environment functioning at Instructional Approach 1.

Profile 2: Applying a Prescriptive Teaching Approach

The teacher, whom we shall call David, had invited a local college professor, a zoologist, to visit the class and teach about local animals (the school was in a mountain community). The class size was 30+, typically too many students. Children sat at tables—the tables acted as dividers for the rows of chairs. The professor came equipped with new technology. From his portable computer, he projected a brief video onto a large screen. Students were fascinated. He had also brought 15 local animals that had been stuffed, including gerbils, gophers, and lizards. Both adults stood at the front of the classroom, with the teacher standing off to the side in a more or less advisory and supervisory pose.

After a brief introductory presentation, the professor distributed the animals among the children, who were now invited to ask questions. Students began to talk to each other as they explored their specimen, and soon hands went up everywhere. Questions tumbled out so fast that students interrupted before the professor could answer a question. It did not take long before both the professor and teacher became visibly annoyed at the disruptions and obvious lack of respect.

The teacher halted the entire process, beginning with, "I am ashamed of you." He identified specific student behaviors, such as general lack of courtesy, raised voices, and interruptions. Almost as a punishment, he suggested that two or three students focus on one animal and collect their questions so that one group at a time could gather the questions and, perhaps more politely, ask them.

Commentary on Profile 2

Looking at this classroom from a brain-based perspective, we believe that more could have been done, and we will explain how when we explore the next two instructional approaches. The brain/mind principles tell us that these children were executing their

curiosity is this

most precious gift, their search for meaning. We know it as curiosity, and it is what the brain does naturally. Our question would automatically be, "How could this teacher have taken better advantage of the brain's tendency to make sense of its experiences?"

The person observing the lesson interviewed the teacher after the class. The teacher was frustrated and angry, apologizing for the students' behavior. The teacher confirmed that students had lost out on the learning he had intended for the professor to provide. This loss was linked to the pressure of time, which the numerous interruptions had shortened. The idea that students were behaving naturally struck him as idealistic. He did not clearly articulate his own notions about student learning, and we determined that they were experience bound and unexamined. Although we discussed alternative approaches and specific strategies, David believed that student behavior would not have allowed for these types of changes. He thought student behavior was the primary problem. We concluded that although different teaching strategies would have been helpful in bringing about some changes in teaching, significant change depended upon much more than change in those areas.

What is critical about this way of thinking or this theory-in-use is that it is prescriptive. Teachers of this type look for something to do to the student; they search for techniques, advice, and strategies that work. Although this approach was inevitably encouraged in teacher training, it is also based on the teacher's own experiences as a learner.

Instructional Approach 1 and the Educational System

The system creates and compounds the problem of stand-and-deliver teaching. Teachers are part of the system, which has a set of expectations and ways of ensuring that those expectations are met. Teachers are expected to give grades, control their students by staying in charge, teach the way the state and district specify, put in a specific number of hours, and abide by union-negotiated rules. Their world is created and perpetuated by an interlocking play of beliefs, expectations, and values negotiated through the interactions of many interest groups, including parents, businesses, taxpayers, and politicians. What we have is a system in which Instructional Approach 1 is deeply entrenched. That context is where teachers are asked to function, and much of teacher education develops and maintains that system. We include in this type of system an emphasis on teaching to specified objectives, using lesson plans that organize down-to-the-minute delivery lessons, and controlling behavior. That teachers then implement a similar instructional approach is hardly surprising.

Instructional Approach 2

This approach is more complex than Instructional Approach 1. Although, like Instructional Approach 1, it is primarily a command-and-control mode of instruction, with many of the same beliefs and practices, some critical differences do exist. The teacher uses complex materials; incorporates powerful and engaging experiences; and focuses on creating meaning, not just memorizing information. This approach also requires a fundamental change in classroom management because students are encouraged to experiment and explore more freely. Instructional Approach 2 requires a move toward mutual respect within a collaborative community.

Perhaps the clearest description of what we mean by Instructional Approach 2 is found in the Third International Math and Science Study (Stedman 1997). In this international study, researchers found that teachers in the countries with the highest scores on the math and science exams tended to differ from U.S. teachers in significant ways. For example, teachers in the countries scoring highest in math (Singapore, Japan, Belgium, and the Slovak Republic) and science (Singapore, Japan, Hungary, and Belgium) tended to focus on depth, particularly the exploration and explication of concepts. In contrast, U.S. teachers tended to have a large number of topics to cover. Students in the top-scoring countries were frequently challenged to see more connections to other subjects or to ask more sophisticated questions; in the United States, the curriculum tended to be fragmented, so that more integrated complex questions were all too often restricted to a limited and prescribed content. And finally, U.S. teachers had an overall lower level of content knowledge (technical/scholastic knowledge).

These observations parallel our own. We believe that a shift from Instructional Approach 1 to Instructional Approach 2 is the necessary next step for most of education. Also, for most people, mastering Instructional Approach 3 without being competent at Instructional Approach 2 is almost impossible.

Objectives of Instruction

• The teacher uses a highly focused set of outcomes, tending to combine prescribed curriculum with instructional activities and prepared materials, such as the FOSS materials (Lawrence Hall of Science 1992).

• Student purposes are secondary.

• From a brain-based learning perspective, the goal is students' acquiring scholastic or technical knowledge. The teacher emphasizes understanding ideas and concepts but often needs help grasping how concepts are translated to real-life experiences.

• Applying the brain/mind principles, we find that this type of instruction can be taken further by enriching the link between specific ideas; linking concepts to real-life experiences; allowing for student-initiated projects; and making subject areas meaningful by engaging students in a search for purpose and meaning.

Teacher Use of Time

Students engage in teacher-orchestrated activities that need a flexible time frame. Attempts to control time, therefore, may cause frustration. Seeing the need to expand artificial time limits beyond 50- to 55-minute periods, the teacher frequently begins to look for greater chunks of time.

Sources for Curriculum and Instruction

Instructional sources are expanded to include groups, discovery, and technology. The teacher provides planned opportunities for student exploration and exchange, and may allow peer teaching. Thematic instruction and the integrated curriculum are introduced but tend to be highly structured.

Teacher Approach to Discipline

The teacher recognizes that students need to develop complex skills, such as listening and the ability to communicate in groups; so group functions are critical as cooperative learning becomes the norm. Failure to cooperate with the teacher-designed plan and activities is seen as disruptive and a problem to maintaining necessary discipline. Students demonstrate self-discipline when activities are provocative and students can relate them to their lives. Creating community is essential to self-organization.

Teacher Approach to Assessment

Assessment usually involves paper-pencil tests and teacher-controlled performance assessments and evaluations. The teacher may experiment with some types of authentic assessment, providing opportunities for problem solving, projects, performance, and student choice of problems and questions. Both teacher and students occasionally develop complex rubrics for evaluation.

Instructional Approach 2 in Action

Teaching at Instructional Approach 2 occurs along a continuum. The more teachers are tied to the Instructional Approach 1 indicators, the more the experiences will resemble direct instructional activities where deeper implications and broader connections to real life are not explored in any depth. As teachers near Instructional Approach 3, such explorations will occur more often. We have observed the widest range in Instructional Approach 2 (from near Instructional Approach 1 to beginning Instructional Approach 3) and provide three examples.

Profile 1: Organizing a Range of Student Activities

A typical example of the beginning of Instructional Approach 2 is a class organized around learning or activity centers. The teacher prepares the materials ahead of time, a task that involves enormous effort. Each center has specific instructions, activities, and objectives, requiring students to complete projects before moving on to the next center. Here is a composite example:

Virginia is well prepared academically to teach history and social studies. Her class is currently studying Rome, and each center deals with a separate aspect of Roman history and civilization. For example, one center focuses on Roman culture, including the fine arts; another, on the geography of the Roman Empire; and another, on daily life, politics, medicine, and architecture. Such centers can be quite elaborate, requiring that students perform varied activities, such as read essential material; engage in structured discussions; create products that summarize their findings (e.g., maps); replicate documents; and dig for artifacts in an artificially constructed dig. Students usually enjoy this type of learning. It has the beginning of complexity because it involves multiple approaches to learning, including student oral and task interactions and multiple sources of instruction.

Profile 2: Using Packaged Materials

Bill is a science and math teacher. His approach differs from Virginia's: He uses packaged materials—purchased and organized sets of materials with teacher instructions and guides for student participation. These materials allow him to create hands-on activities so that students can experience a concept in action. The packages tend to be for specific subjects. For science, Bill uses the FOSS materials (Lawrence Hall of Science 1992); for mathematics, Math Renaissance. He regularly supplements the materials with appropriate academic background.

Bill usually begins each section with an interesting true story that establishes the context and ties concepts to real-life experiences. Then he explains the salient and critical concepts and introduces activities to let students test them. Such activities are usually experiments, exercises, and small projects that require teamwork. When the students are finished, they report on what they did and discovered, discussing concepts, issues, and procedures.

Commentary on Profiles 1 and 2

Note that both teachers still control the delivery of content. The main change from Instructional Approach 1 teachers is that Instructional Approach 2 teachers have begun to incorporate experiences into the teaching, and these experiences generate new possibilities for student-teacher interactions. The teacher, however, still selects and controls the meaning and purpose for the experience. Discipline is still based on student compliance with teacher purpose, and the teacher specifies assessment.

One problem here is that teachers, schools, districts, and states have designated specific topics to be mastered during specified periods of time, all based on a fragmented notion of knowledge. The teachers, therefore, "deliver" this knowledge within clear parameters and limitations, often at the expense of students' search for understanding and connections to their own world. When asked how learning about Romans relates to their own lives, most students are bewildered by the question.

Now let us contrast our first two teachers with a more advanced Instructional Approach 2 teacher.

Profile 3: Introducing Life into Experience

When we first observed Gareth at the beginning of our school partnership, she was a sophisticated Instructional Approach 1 teacher who loved teaching. She knew as much about her subject as most college professors, and she tried to teach like one to 7th graders. They genuinely liked her and followed her instructions. Everything was clearly spelled out, and students had the opportunity to practice what she showed them. Even then, we could see her deep need to communicate, but it came out as explanations in one form or another. From our observations, students did as they were told and scored well, but meaning and generalization were rare.

Here is Gareth two and a half years later teaching about adjectives. As we walk into the class, she is telling a mundane and boring story. She asks the students about the story, and they confirm our impression. She next switches to an animated story (her invention) about a tree that escaped from the back lot of the school.

"It pulled out its roots, up out of the mucky soil, and began to run down the road."

She continues to embellish the story and finally comes to a halt. Students are mesmerized, listening half laughing, half fascinated. She asks them to identify the difference between the first and second story. Comments include, "you used more descriptive words," "more colorful words," "the second story was more fun to listen to." She agrees, and after pushing for more specifics, uses their comments to define adjectives, writing the definition on the board.

Next, she pulls out an old plastic waterproof seaman's coat, and after giving a brief history of the coat, asks the students to generate descriptive words or adjectives that describe the coat. Students begin to brainstorm, and she writes their words on the board. She then passes the coat from group to group, asking each to generate more adjectives until the board is almost full.

When they have finished, she says, "You know what? We can take every one of these adjectives and explode them. Let's look at an example. Some of you said that the coat is ugly. How ugly? What type of ugly? Ugly like something else? Like what else?"

Students take a little time to brainstorm. After a few moments, she reminds them of the short stories they have been writing and asks them to find three adjectives in their writing and explode them by making their descriptions more powerful and interesting. Students spend the remaining class time consulting with each other and giving suggestions. The teacher acts as a resource, going around to as many students as possible.

Commentary on Profile 3

This learning is teacher controlled, based on prescribed and organized content, and has specific outcomes and assessments. It is Instructional Approach 2 because it uses different types of complex experiences and emphasizes teaching concepts as well as facts and skills. Concepts are critical for engaging higher-order thinking, and mastering concepts is one of the greatest benefits of this type of teaching.

It is advanced Instructional Approach 2 because students are constructing their own connections—teacher instruction alone does not determine the entire path and focus of the lesson. The approach to time is also different. Gareth cannot tell ahead of time how long her students will take to dialogue with her. She must be flexible, and since at this time she was in an Instructional Approach 1 school, she had to leave for tomorrow's class whatever a natural flow would have created, led by students' natural exploration of writing and guided by their interests.

Perhaps most important is that both the teacher and students are engaged in an evolving and creative process that provides meaning and opportunities for applying what students are learning to their own products. Given the question of, "Why are you learning this?" these students will answer something like, "I want to write my short story and this helps me." The purpose for their work is clearer. Also, for schools to move into flexible scheduling, teachers need to understand how to teach using Instructional Approach 2.

Instructional Approach 2 and the Educational System

Instructional Approach 2 teachers can implement thematic instruction, cooperative learning, and hands-on science or math, provided these can be incorporated into orthodox time periods and have publicly supported objectives and modes of assessment. The emphasis is on giving teachers specific strategies and instructions, which they can follow, practice, and rehearse on their own. Instructional Approach 2 does not disrupt the school, district, and state mandates or deviate from traditional teaching enough to generate too much uncertainty or garner negative community or system reactions.

Instructional Approach 2 teachers, as we have seen in Gareth's focus on adjectives, can be creative and move beyond packaged teacher materials to include teacher creativity. They can also use technology but not in the free-flowing, open-space format so compatible with a futuristic view.

Instructional Approach 3

This approach is the most learner centered of the approaches—genuine student interest is at its core. Based on the view that people learn naturally, it is highly organic and dynamic, with experiences that approach the complexity of real life. The language and methods of Instructional Approach 3 teachers are often considered suspect and nontraditional by others.

Instructional Approach 3 in Action

Instructional Approach 3 incorporates Instructional Approaches 1 and 2 in the sense that it includes elements of direct instruction. What is remarkable, however, is the flow and sense of naturalness or wholeness that confronts the observer.

A Profile: Engaging Students in Learning

Doris is an elementary school teacher. At the time of this observation, she is part of a school that provides inservice training on whole language to teachers. They come on Fridays and quietly observe teaching in designated classrooms. They then meet that evening and the following Saturday to discuss questions and to focus on skill development.

On this particular day (Thursday), one of us happens to be in the back of the class as she looks at her 3rd grade students and says, "I have a problem. Tomorrow I need to get 50 people into this classroom. I need to know how many tables to get and where to place them so that everyone can participate. Do you think we can work on this problem?"

Hands go up everywhere. With her guidance, students divide into research teams who will solve the puzzle. They agree that the team with the best answer will have its solution adopted.

Students begin the puzzle, draw diagrams, and take measurements. They are allowed into the classroom during breaks and at lunch time to measure the size of the room, tables, and chairs. They attempt to diagram their solution. In the afternoon, after they present the solutions and discuss the pros and cons, the entire class selects the best solution and Doris adopts their choice.

Commentary on the Profile

How does this profile illustrate Instructional Approach 3? The classroom is a highly sophisticated, collaborative community. Low threat/high challenge is a way of life. Students take responsibility for almost all areas of physically organizing the classroom. Everyone has a responsibility, from being in charge of the windows, to cleaning the carpets when necessary, to returning errant insects back to nature. Students organize into cooperative groups and pairs, or work by themselves as needed. They are also involved in their own assessment as they spell out what they plan to improve. They are used to getting feedback and comments on their presentations and accomplishments from Doris and their fellow students. Along with Doris, they decide how best to explore a concept or learn something new. Everyone asks questions and challenges answers. Scientific thinking is encouraged at all times, as is spontaneity. Other adults have often remarked on how different these students are. Most of them are naturally polite and self-sufficient. It is their belief in their own agency that sets them apart.

Continuation of the Profile

On another occasion, the day of the inservice training (when small groups visit actual classrooms), Doris's room was again different and reflected student planning. Rather than having teachers stand in the back of the room and observe what went on, as was customary, the class was set up so that desks were in pairs, with an empty desk next to each student. Each adult visitor was then escorted by a student to an empty desk until desks were full, so that the entire class consisted of children and adults working together. Two students sat at the front, and Doris was at her table in the back.

Students ran the first activity. They asked everyone to write a short description about an experience from the preceding day. Adults and children participated. All names—students and visitors—had been written on small pieces of paper and placed in a box. The students at the front did a blind drawing of names, and those selected were asked to come to the front and read aloud what they had written. Again, both adults and children participated. After each person had finished, the class asked questions. The session ended when Doris sensed that students were becoming restless, and she took a vote on whether to continue and for how long. And so the day went. . . .

Continuation of the Profile Commentary

Note here the integration of children and adults so that adults became natural models, the empowerment of the students as they led the session, and Doris's use of an inservice day to educate students. She used a structure and routines, but did not need to exercise control. Doris also felt free to answer visitors' questions about what she was doing, and the students were privy to those conversations. Note also that a substantial amount of practice was built into the process, but that each time was different enough so that it did not become boring.

Examples of Instructional Approach 3 in the higher grades are available. One is the Creative Learning Plaza (see Caine and Caine 1997), a high-tech environment for about 150 upper-grade students, where the work is built around complex projects and teachers tend to be roving facilitators. Short sessions on specific topics in an Instructional Approach 2 mode are employed as needed.

Other complex projects, which engage students around the world in interactive research, also exemplify Instructional Approach 3. See, for instance, the Space Islands Project (Johnson 1995).

5

Investigating the Foundations of the Instructional Approaches

I want for my students the opposite of what I got in school. Passive, docile, well-behaved, I managed to spirit through my early education unseen and untouched. I had no say as to what I read, wrote, or thought about. Speaking up was beyond conception. The teacher's point of view, narrow, in that it was that of a single individual, was the only active voice in the classroom. I was a successful student, by measure of my grades; but I remember coming away from highly anticipated topics of study feeling deflated and let down. I was happy when school got out, so I could go home to the exciting real world of life in my own backyard. There, the birds we had studied at school—flat, paper, lifeless, and songless—actually lived, foraged, and flew, filling my soul with their songs.

—Doris Lombard
Elementary School Teacher, Idyllwild School

The above quote is from what we identify as an Instructional Approach 3 teacher. Doris has the kind of flow in her classroom, along with the necessary orderliness and coherence, that we were looking for. Most teachers, however, would find this flow intolerable. As one

61

admiring colleague of hers put it: "She's brilliant, but I always feel I want to go in there [her class] and pick things up and straighten things out."

In our opinion, the human brain learns best in complex environments that are as naturally rich as possible. But living on the edge of possibility while keeping a sense of orderliness is very, very challenging. The question is, how is it done? In this chapter, we explain the process we used to try to answer that question—a process that led to our identifying what we now call perceptual orientations.

Identifying the perceptual orientations was possible largely because of our approach to research. Such an approach could be compared to a hermeneutic process that resembled a spiral: Our understandings were continually tested, altered, and reexamined.

From the beginning, we were determined to be open to our combined experiences. We relished uncertainty whenever and however it surfaced. We welcomed those things that made no immediate sense, given our understandings and expectations. Moreover, we felt free to interpret data from continued readings in a broad range of fields. We also relied on the lens of our own experiences to ask questions, challenge collective thinking, and find possible answers.

A Teacher Questionnaire to Dig Deeper

As discussed in Chapter 3, our observations, interviews, and work with our teachers had given us a clear sense that distinct differences in mental models influenced how teachers taught. Next we wondered if these differences could surface in another way and if there was anything more to them. We therefore developed a questionnaire (see Figure 5.1 on p. 63) that we hoped would allow these differences between instructional approaches to emerge.

As we observed teachers and analyzed their responses to the questionnaire, we found patterns of beliefs and ways of looking at the world that appeared to provide a larger context within which the mental models of learning and teaching were formed and embedded. These underlying patterns eventually became known as Perceptual Orientations 1, 2, and 3; each represents a type of world view.

FIGURE 5.1

QUESTIONNAIRE TO HELP IDENTIFY DIFFERENCES AMONG INSTRUC-TIONAL APPROACHES

1. When you are teaching, what decisions about what you actually do in your classroom do you believe others govern and what decisions do you feel free to make yourself? Please list.

2. Where do the ideas for your teaching come from?

3. How do you organize your ideas for teaching? How do time parameters influence your planning?

4. How do you assure student empowerment?

5. Do you see a difference between an activity and an experience? How would you describe that difference?

6. Do you ever deviate from the prescribed curriculum? If so, under what circumstances?

7. What does order in your class mean? How do you maintain order?

8. What is your approach to grading and evaluation? Please be specific.

9. How do you accommodate student interests and needs? Please give examples.

10. How do you help your students "consolidate" what they are learning?

11. Do you observe, monitor, and assess your own teaching and learning? When? How?

12. How do you create low threat-high challenge?

13. Teaching linked to real-life experiences can have an open-ended quality because there is no one correct answer. How can teachers teach this way without feeling a loss of control over students and what they need to learn?

We first gave the questionnaire to the teachers in our schools. Then we branched out and gave it to any schools and teachers willing to fill it out. We included the entire K–12 range of teachers, as well as urban, suburban, and low-income schools, and schools for the gifted and talented. Including teachers in our schools, 161 educators filled it out and returned it.

We were looking for answers that would provide clues about the teacher's actual in-class behavior and the underlying beliefs or assumptions that guided the teacher's work. In other words, we were looking for their approach to time, discipline, and assessment, and for instructional sources and type of instruction used. And we were also looking for beliefs related to these behaviors.

We did find clear patterns indicating different instructional approaches. Thus, teachers who used Instructional Approach 3 are often more likely to be in agreement with someone at another school, across the United States, or across the state, rather than with someone in their own school. Yet these teachers are often unable to explain their approach to teaching and tend to be regarded as different. They certainly break many of the rules of tradition that the average teacher adheres to.

Instructional Approach 3 teaching requires a different kind of thinking. These teachers are different sorts of people. And it is their thinking, not just their approach to teaching, that organizes what they do. They can use all three instructional approaches, for example, but their choice of when and where these are used is extremely flexible and based upon a contextual perspective.

An essential difference in Instructional Approach 3 teachers is their ability to "think out of the box." They have an open systems instructional approach: They believe that much of what happens in life outside the formal boundaries of education is relevant to their job. Moreover, the ways in which they function in the classroom reflect a fundamental, albeit intuitive, belief that their classrooms are complex adaptive systems rather than mechanical systems.

Questionnaire Responses and Interpretations

A sampling of teacher responses to the questionnaire highlights and contrasts the three instructional approaches and the perceptual orientations. The responses represent the thinking that marks each instructional approach. Occasionally, we supplement the questionnaire responses with others, such as those offered by teachers we interviewed at the Illinois Math and Science Academy and by teachers we worked with outside the two schools we have identified.

Most responses were anonymous, but sometimes, especially with Instructional Approach 3 teachers, we added classroom observation or interviews. At the end of each response is a letter indicating whether the respondent was in an elementary school (E), middle school (M), or high school (HS). We limit our report to K–12 teachers, but additional informal data suggest that these differences also apply at the university level.

Question 2: "Where do the ideas for your teaching come from?"

Instructional Approach 1 Responses

Instructional Approach 1 teachers tend to get their ideas from traditional, external sources (as opposed to internally generated or creative ideas), and a few admitted to using lessons over again from year to year. Here are some examples:

> [Response 1]
> The IEP [individual education plan] (I have most feed-in to that) is based on other standardized scores. It controls academic goals (M).

> [Response 2]
> First, I look through my resources—making notes about books, pages, etc. Then I make copies of all these resources and ideas and put them together in a folder or notebook. From these notes and pages, I make my weekly, monthly, lesson plans—sometimes, in a move of desperation, I just go through my resources and make my lesson plans. I have most of my books, texts, etc., at home. They are arranged on bookshelves or in piles that pertain to a particular curriculum area (E).

Instructional Approach 2 Responses

Instructional Approach 2 teachers conduct a broader search for ideas. They see themselves in charge of creating lessons that are interesting and varied. They see themselves as the experts searching for the necessary enriching ideas and materials that will help them create activities that interest students. They are also searching for materials and inservice programs that provide strategies that work.

Some have begun to value depth over breadth of coverage (concepts over facts).

As with Instructional Approach 1, the sources for their ideas fall within the range of educational resources that help them improve their teaching. Some teachers use a great deal of creativity to create challenging, entertaining lessons—which turn out to be an enormous amount of work. They see themselves as making learning happen. They are pushing the limits of the status quo while staying very much within it. Viewing themselves as the experts who lead the instruction, they do all the searching, and they feel responsible for what students do and how they do it. In our terms, they focus heavily on teaching technical/scholastic knowledge. Responses in the Instructional Approach 2 range include the following:

[Response 1]
My ideas come from a wide variety of resources. Including textbook and supplements, most activities I have sought out and purchased. Creative writing ideas and help in that area are given to me by my team members. I attend a lot of workshops on my own time to develop more creative open-ended activities for students (M).

[Response 2]
The ideas for my teaching come from anywhere and everywhere. I'm quite open to, and am always looking for, new, interesting, and motivating ways of teaching. I look through educational books and magazines, brainstorm with other teachers, and attend conferences. I'm always looking for and trying to create new ideas of how to teach (E).

[Response 3]
[My ideas come from the following:] *Math Their Way Manual and Newsletter; Math Excursions—K; Explorations—K; Developing Number Concepts Manual* and other math resource books; *Houghton Mifflin Literature Manual; FOSS Science Kits; Here's Looking At You 2000 Ret.; Health and Safety Binder; Social Studies— Silver Burdette;* variety of resource materials; exchange of ideas with colleagues; inservice programs and conferences; study groups; brainstorming—to make learning experiences experiential; and state frameworks and district grade-level expectations (E).

Instructional Approach 3 Responses

Little prepared us for the responses from Instructional Approach 3 teachers. They were totally different. Here are some examples:

[Response 1]
Ideas come from every facet of my life. Walking in the forest, open to the beauty around me, the smell of the sun-baked pine needles, the sight of the full moon rising over silhouetted mountains, such things keep me open to the creative forces of nature. During the meditative state as I perform the routines of living, showering, or weeding in my garden, perhaps an insight will inspire a new approach to try. When I am in the flow of the activities and interactions at school, possibilities occur to me. Conversations, or just being in the presence of certain expansive personalities, energizes me, helping me to crystallize my thoughts (E).

[Response 2]
I have always felt like a sponge. Sometimes they come to me in a bookstore while browsing, often on trips to historical sites, sometimes and very, very frequently while reading the newspapers. I read four newspapers a day. Lately, I have been getting some fantastic ideas over the Internet. For example, I was able to take oral histories from an SPA project from the 1930s and wed this with maps and diaries from still other sources on the 'Net (HS).

[Response 3]
They also come from virtually anything I do. Films, events, personal interactions, jogging, dancing, drinking, eating, reading—are all potential areas for teaching ideas. Many of the most successful ideas have come from student reactions to implemented ideas, either in terms of refining, enlarging, or eliminating (HS).

[Response 4]
My ideas just come to me in the middle of instruction and at home when I'm not consciously thinking about school. Many ideas come as I explain to others what I have done, what worked, and what didn't. This seems to help things gel. Our discussions always lead to more ideas and clarification. The kids in my classroom also offer great ideas. I have to constantly watch for where their interest lies (E).

The language that Instructional Approach 3 teachers use is flowing and more global. One is struck by the almost total absence of reference to formal instructional input on how to teach the content. These are bright teachers who somehow do not limit the source of knowledge to a program, technique, or any single approach. Few boundaries are between their everyday world and teaching. A lived connectedness between life experience and what goes on in the classroom is present. With it is a comprehension that the curriculum reflects real life and is embedded everywhere, and that nonlinearity is the norm. We see reference to student needs and interests; student ideas are a primary source and focus of instruction. Empowering others is central.

Our initial conclusions and design had not prepared us for such profound differences in thinking. Clearly, these teachers had a wide capacity to synthesize and integrate disparate information. They lived in a world that was rich with possibility. They could consistently see the relevance to themselves and their work within a wide range of experiences. And they could call upon new ideas without planning, on a moment-by-moment basis. Thus, many features of complex adaptive systems seemed to be present—at home with disequilibrium, flexibility, self-reference, and self-organization. These features are what made possible their handling a more prolific flow of information.

These types of responses led to our reexamining our notion of instructional approaches. Our original notion was far too limited to describe what we were observing. Even though Instructional Approach 3 thinkers often used methodologies that could be described on the surface as Instructional Approach 1 or Instructional Approach 2, clear differences in their thinking and in what they did with those strategies were apparent. Those differences were what we began to look for and why we created the distinction between instructional approaches and perceptual orientations.

Question 3: "How do you organize your ideas for teaching? How do time parameters influence your planning?"

Instructional Approach 1 Responses

A primary indication of Instructional Approach 1 is the teachers' acceptance of the mandated schedule. It is never questioned. Instructional Approach 1 teachers diligently seek to make the 55-minute lesson structure work. We were struck by the teachers' mechanistic ordering of the tasks and content. Even when the teachers refer to student interests, they interpret those interests within the context of the goals the system prescribes. Despite reference to learning styles, multiple intelligences, or group work (elements of an espoused theory), the teaching plan fragments learning and subsumes student meanings. To understand their approach, we need to get away from the teachers' language and look at their action or at the concepts that are directly linked to action. Here are some sample responses:

[Response 1]
When planning a unit, I look at time allowances given by lesson. Usually I determine about how much can be covered in a 55-minute period, due to learning styles and limitations of students (previous experience, knowledge levels, learning disabilities). I will give more or less time as needed. I have come to learn that rigid schedules do not work! (M). [Note: Despite this last sentence, which we see as the espoused theory, the teacher adheres strictly to 55-minute lessons.]

[Response 2]
I routinely use the lesson plan format, working on one subject area for a one- to two-week period. After working on math (for example), I go onto another subject, integrating the activities as is possible (E).

[Response 3]
By topic. I study the topic and decide what language components and structures I will need to teach in order for the students to become proficient in the topic. For example, to describe what their daily life routine entails would require a teaching and mastery of (a) reflexive verbs; (b) food; (c) vocabulary, etc. (HS).

Instructional Approach 2 Responses

Instructional Approach 2 thinkers clearly feel constrained by pre-scribed blocks of 55 minutes. They would like larger amounts of time and opportunities to go beyond the rigid schedule. They understand that ideas and experiences are complex and need to be explored. At the same time, teachers remain in charge of what is selected, when time will be available for students' interests, and how activities that cover the required topics can be scheduled. A taken-for-granted belief that teachers control "how things should be" within a larger context is implicit. Here are some responses:

[Response 1]
Time parameters are a difficult issue in my science class. Labs and activities are often cut off or hurried to fit in with present class time blocks. I believe this affects continuity. I deviate from the prescribed curriculum whenever I feel that my students will gain new insight, a better understanding of the world around them, and their responsibilities. For example, when I am teaching a subject and am presented with high student interest on a side issue, I will spend time with them answering their questions. Format of how we seek answers to their questions depends on available materials (M).

[Response 2]
On Mondays, Tuesdays, and Wednesdays, we explore together high-interest facts. We read, discuss, and research. On Thursdays and Fridays, we have high-interest exploration, where children and adults are free to explore what interests them. I am still working on organizing my ideas. When I am organized, the organization constantly changes (E). [Note: This response reveals the beginning elements of Instructional Approach 3.]

Instructional Approach 3 Responses

Instructional Approach 3 has a fundamentally different dynamic interaction with time. Teachers show flexibility, play with possibilities, and are comfortable with uncertainty. In one answer, a teacher acknow-ledges an "uncomfortable zone," which mirrors the edge of chaos where complex adaptive systems thrive—and which we have translated as living on the edge of possibility.

Another answer reveals a sense of long-term personal changes, which are perceived to affect learning and instruction here and now. Often, teachers refer to planning for greater "chunks" of time. In our view, Instructional Approach 3 teachers feel free to explore the curriculum more fully, while still showing a strong sense of responsibility and adhering to orderly processes. This type of teacher believes that when purpose, skill, and context are aligned, the situation can actually be allowed to take care of itself, and that good, complex learning will naturally result. Here are some responses to interviews and the questionnaire:

[Response 1]
Well, what I've done is I've looked at the framework along with our district guidelines, and I've laid out a plan, especially with the multi-age [class], because you are meeting so many different needs and when the class . . . we originally took off on water in my classroom. We were learning about where water comes from, where our drinking water comes from, and where our water goes when it goes down the drain. Because that was something that needed to be covered. And from there, that's when the children got excited about water and oceans and the whole thing there. I took them to the library to find books about water. They came back with books about the ocean. So then when I realized we were going to the ocean, I looked at the framework, I looked at the guidelines, and I said, "Okay, what can I teach while we still do this?" So we talked about whale migration—so we've looked at maps. We've talked about islands with coral reefs—so we've looked at land forms, and it's easy to incorporate in the reading, the writing, and the spelling. Mostly it's looking at science. We've done a lot of things with sink and float. We did a quart investigation to learn how to measure quarts and how standard measurement has come into our lives to play such an important role. And so you just kind of look at, okay, what can I do? Where can I plug it in and it just kind of happens? (E)

[Response 2]
Time parameters are always somewhat of a problem. Particularly, I discover with certain types of bright students that they simply wish to surf the problem and then go on to something new and

different. It is difficult to teach them discipline and how to mine data and play with ideas in fostering creativity (HS).

[Response 3]
Frankly, I am reluctant to say, organization of ideas is so free flowing that it approaches chaos. In an uncomfortable zone between, "I know we'll get there," and "but, I'm not sure where we're going," I pursue my visions of learning, sometimes leading, sometimes following the lead of the youngsters (E).

[Response 4]
Chronologically, thematically (visually, intellectually, by sound, etc.), around specific [curriculum requirements] but still limited by the 50- 100-minute time slots (HS).

[Response 5]
I am nowhere near the mathematician I was. In fact, I don't really care as much about solving the problems; but I am a much better problem poser. When I see a problem now, the problem 10 years ago would have intrigued me to want to sit down and solve it. I am not as interested in solving a problem. As a matter of fact, when I look at a problem, I no longer probably focus on, "Gee, if I do this, it might work out and I could solve it." Rather, I immediately look at the problem and say, "What variations or twists can I put on that problem to create new ones?" (HS).

[Response 6]
Sometimes I get nervous because I don't have a prepared lesson as I go into class. I mean, I literally don't know what to say next. But then the students ask me a question or show me what they're doing, and we're off and running. I do have a focus, even a pretty worked out long-term plan, but there is no minute-to-minute predictability. The students and I create that—the moment— together (M).

In a video interview of a Dry Creek K–1 teacher, we asked, "How do you come up with lesson plans in brain-based learning?" Here is the response:

Lesson plans are much different with what I'm doing than they were in the past. There's no rigid schedule. It's not from 8 to 9:00 we'll do spelling; from 9 to 10:00, we'll do reading and so on. It's, okay, in the morning, let's talk, let's do some math stuff. In the afternoon, let's do some reading stuff. Or maybe a whole day you might spend on math. When we were doing a quartz exploration, we spent a week on math. There was reading and other things involved, but the major focus of that week was quartz exploration and math. So, you're looking more at the big picture instead of small fragments when you are planning. So our plans are probably a month long, and they are not rigid, and they change every day (E).

What we find striking here is that despite the absence of specific scheduling and predictable lesson plans, teachers use a sort of dynamic patterning in which content and time interact and swirl around student interests, so that curriculum is covered but not in a preordained way. In our view, this patterning is exactly like the patterns of order found in complex adaptive systems at the edge of possibility. These patterns are described in terms of attractors or basins of attraction. They are messy and, in a sense, unplanned, yet they clearly have a form and a movement that engages the students and leads to complex learning. Indeed, this flow and patterning can only be sustained with sufficient dynamism. Meeting this need is why we see all these teachers consistently engaging current student interests and then using active processing in its various forms to keep the movement going. Once again, the language used appears vague and imprecise. But precision is evident in moment-to-moment actions and interventions with students. These teachers cannot tell us what they are going to do or what the precise organization of their lessons is because the class as a whole determines this work. A much better question to ask them is what they would like students to understand and why this understanding is important for them. We began to see how technology would be critical for these classrooms.

Questions 4 and 7: "How do you assure student empowerment?" "What does order in your class mean? How do you maintain order?"

Instructional Approach 1 Responses

Although the following comments may appear exaggerated, in our experience, they reflect the discipline policy for over 90 percent of the classrooms we observed. Teachers define misbehavior as violations of rules that they establish; the rules represent what the larger system expects. Correct behavior is then enforced by a variety of possible sanctions. Behavior needs to be controlled, and power tied to some form of coercion is used to maintain control. Students may have some say, but teachers establish the context in which such discussions occur. Behavior modification plans thrive at Instructional Approach 2. Here are some responses:

> [Response 1]
> Lab and activity rules are covered before students begin. Off-task and disruptive behaviors waste everyone's time and are dealt with in a variety of ways:
>
> • Student is given a warning.
> • Lunch detention is assigned and a note is sent home to a parent.
> • Student may be moved and lose privileges if behavior continues.
> • Student and I sit down and come up with a plan to solve problems.
> • Parent conferences in person or by phone are held.
> • I consult with other team members and use ideas they suggest. We have had team meetings with parents and a student when the student has severe problems in all classes.
> • If none of the above works, suspension from class is given (M).

> [Response 2]
> Order—students engaged in work—on task—not disrupting others (HS).

Instructional Approach 2 Responses

Some of these responses read like Instructional Approach 3, showing how difficult drawing boundaries is. The reason for defining these responses as Instructional Approach 2 is that they show a clear hierarchy dominating instruction. An almost subliminal hand is on the reins about what is permissible to do or cover and who has the power to control tasks and timing, both related to evaluation. This hand on the reins is found in the qualifying language, such as, "As I prepare lessons."

What we are looking for now in teachers' thinking is very subtle—a grasp of self-generated and self-sustaining order, which allows order, dynamism, and self-organization to prevail. That order is found in Instructional Approach 3 teachers and occasionally in Instructional Approach 2 teachers. Here are some examples of the latter:

[Response 1]
Students are given the opportunity to share in the decision-making process. Students are listened to. Democratic processes are in place. All students have opportunities for leadership: cooperative groups, student experts, panels, cross-age tutors, student success teacher, and grade leadership teams (E).

[Response 2]
Student empowerment and alternative learning styles are addressed in teaching information. Students are encouraged to expand and push to their highest abilities on assignments. Students are welcome to ask to present information in a different format than offered. They are often asked to brainstorm ways of presenting information learned. Students are usually given the opportunity of working in groups they have chosen (M).

Instructional Approach 3 Responses

The first point is that Instructional Approach 3 does not mean laissez-faire. Teachers have a clear sense of their responsibilities and purposes. The second point is that teachers perceive a link among maintaining order, recognizing student interests, and allowing student choices. Thus, by empowering students to express their opinions and then by allowing the class to move in the direction of those interests and opinions, teachers turn what could be disruption into a form of energy that holds students' attention. Teachers therefore utilize not only structured democratic procedures but also the life in the classroom as a source of orderliness. The system of rules and consequences is not abandoned; it is secondary—the fallback system. Self-organization is primary and based on meaningful work and purposeful projects, which both encourage and require self-efficacy. The following responses exemplify this self-organization:

[Response 1]

Q. Anything else you would like to add that we haven't talked about?

A. The one thing that I would like to add is when you go into a classroom where students are learning in a BBL [brain-based learning] environment, they are engaged in learning. They are totally immersed. You are not going to see students that are off task. They're going to be so engrossed with what they are doing that they're not going to look for something else to do. And if they do, their group or the students around them are going to go on without them, and nobody wants to be left behind. It's something that totally engrosses the learner. Each learner finds something— one bit, one part—that's really important to them and they go from there and that's where they begin sharing their different ideas (Videotaped Interview with Teacher from Dry Creek Elementary School).

The remaining responses are from the questionnaire and interviews:

[Response 2]

Everyone is needed. Everyone has an important contribution to make, as to the successful functioning of our classroom. The bottom line is that we all respect each other and behave in accordingly appropriate manners. As social skills progress, students use verbal conflict resolution techniques, telling what bothers them, and offering an alternate behavior: "Marie, I don't like it when you put your stuff all over my desk. Please keep it on your own desk." Persistent problems are written, dated, signed, and handed to the offending party to sign that they read it, and to write their side of it, or an apology, if so desired. I keep these "Personal Problem" accounts for my own reference. The students are empowered to recognize and respect their own feelings, to expect respect from others, and to ask for it if it is not given, all of which is challenging in this real world of name calling and violence (E).

[Response 3]
Feedback and input from the students are the forces that both propel and steer much of the learning that goes on in our classroom. Having an active say about how much more time is needed to complete a project as we would like to complete it empowers and challenges. Creating the spelling word list and designating the words as below, at, or above grade level empower and challenge. Having ample time to process and write on topics of individual choice, knowing an attentive, appreciative audience awaits, ready with compliments, questions, or suggestions, is empowering and challenging (E).

[Response 4]
Student empowerment is, in part, a by-product of child-centered, self-selected activities and long-range projects that cross curriculums. A teacher must also be in tune with what sparks genuine interest in their students and be willing to drop preplanned agendas and go where students want to go. You have to listen to their ideas and let them try to make it work. You must put them in the position of "teacher" as often as possible. You must pose broad questions, accept all answers, and encourage students to demonstrate the how and why (E).

[Response 5]
Tricky. Nonverbal as well as verbal feedback tells me a lot. On the other hand, I no longer subscribe to the belief that students should run the curriculum and we should only study what they wish to study. A good and effective teacher should be able to interest and empower students in concepts, ideas, and units that they didn't know could interest them. After all, that is one of the key roles of the teacher (IIS).

[Response 6]
What does order in your class mean. I don't even know how to respond. . . . I just say, student and teacher have respect for each other and the learning process takes care of that (HS).

What we find is that the natural order that unfolds in the pursuit of learning becomes the order that replaces most traditional approaches to discipline. A discipline policy, with rules and sanctions requiring teachers to exercise power and control, becomes more important when we separate learning from discipline. When we have an internally coherent dynamic where everything is connected, orderliness becomes a property or feature of how the whole system works.

Implicit within this willingness to go where student interests lead or to engage student interest in new concepts and ideas is a broad grasp of the curriculum. Such a grasp is another aspect of what we later came to call broad cognitive horizons (see Chapter 7). Teachers know opportunities to introduce all the prescribed material will arise, so they do not need to panic about losing an opportunity for a specific lesson. That awareness is what frees them from making students behave properly so that they are ready for what must be covered next. It also indicates a broader grasp of content and the unfolding of learning than is found in Instructional Approaches 1 and 2. Broad cognitive horizons allow for a felt meaning for, and comfort with, process.

Question 8: "What is your approach to grading and evaluation? Please be specific."

Responses to this question clearly reveal the distinction between the two paradigms. Mechanistic thinking carries with it using feedback and control to induce specific outcomes. Those who carry the spirit of complex adaptive systems in their minds use feedback to further animate the process and help participants monitor themselves so that they can become more capable and competent. For these teachers, feedback is constant, not just a culminating activity. Instructional Approach 1 evaluations are based on quantifiable data tied to specific tests or documents that teachers or an external agent designs, with criteria that are also external to student goals, purposes, and meanings.

Instructional Approach 1 Response

This response demonstrates how externally established criteria determine student effort. Even though the following quote mentions portfolios, for example, work completed is for the teacher to evaluate. Student evaluation is not even considered:

> Effort counts. Look for progress. Four-point system: $A = 4$, $B = 3$, $C = 2$, $D = 1$, F only if there's no effort (I've not given one). . . . Have portfolios. . . . [so I can] see specifically how they tackle work. In science, [we use] drawings and lectures (M).

Instructional Approach 2 Response

Teacher-determined outcomes dictated every method used at Instructional Approach 2. Students invariably assigned primary value to grades. A wide variety of assessments is employed:

- Creative writing that includes science and creativity.
- Presentations (e.g., videotapes; oral programs; skits; songs; poems; and projects, both group and individual).
- Art—encouraged in all written assignments.
- Vocabulary presented through art and drawings.
- Lab write-ups.
- Letter writing.
- Debates.
- Handouts.
- Books made by students covering science facts.

Teachers explain (both orally and in writing) a rubric at the same time they explain directions, so that students know what is expected of them:

> Grades are usually based on
>
> - Science facts.
> - Creativity.
> - Neatness.
> - On time.
> - Art.
> - Presentation.
> - Group grades (when applicable). Students are evaluated on individual effort as well as collaborative effort.
> - Points are given for each area, then total points are added up when I review work (M).

Instructional Approach 3 Responses

Instructional Approach 3 teachers are frustrated by the restriction to using quantifiable assessment that most schools and educational institutions prescribe. To them, learning is literally unbounded. They are always confined by the absence of broad definitions of successful learning, and they welcome alternative modes of assessment. Here are some sample responses:

[Response 1]
Boy, is that a good question, because one of the ways we try to do it is by de-emphasizing traditional grading procedures. We try to take and convince students that we are not very much interested in the whole idea of grading their performance. What we're interested in is monitoring their progress from where they are when they come in to where they are when they come out as far as what they can do in some of these broad areas we are talking about. We try to get explicit about what some of those areas are:

• Can you look at a situation and in fact identify a problem that needs solving? Can you find the problem in it?
• Can you take a huge set of information and extract the most important relevant data in the information that is going to be useful for you to take and try to deal with a problem in the situation you have?
• Can you take something you understand and explain it clearly to someone else?
• Can you take two ideas that don't seem to be connected and find a way to demonstrate to yourself and others that they are in fact connected and have something to do with each other?

Those are the kinds of general examples, the general kinds of things we are looking for students to get better at. We try to take and give them ways of demonstrating that to us. But it's real hard to get clear to them the criteria by which we are judging how successful they are at that. They see the way we're evaluating them as being fundamentally subjective. So there's almost no way we can, with any objective reality, put some kind of scale up against what they are doing. We can tell them they are doing better than before. We can tell them that they are not yet where we want them to be. But we can't tell them if this is a scale from there to there exactly where they are along there. And they have all this background experience saying, "Well, is that a 65 percent or a 70 percent?" or something like that. When we can't do that, they basically tell us, "Well, you're just judging us subjectively."

And the answer we have to that is, "Yea, we are pretty much," but I don't know what else to do with it because I find it difficult to put any kind of real numerical scale on such a thing.

And they get uncomfortable with that because what they generally say is, "Well, then you're just judging me on some sort of subjective criteria. That's not fair."

And in a sense they are right, but I don't know what else to do about it. So the issue with trying to get past grades reduces one kind of threat, but it kind of has another laid on top of it because they feel they are being exposed to some kind of subjective evaluation, which they have little control over (HS).

[Response 2]
We are fortunate to have the difficulty of choosing among degrees of excellence for the most part. As I said, if our students engage the texts, they are empowered and thus pass the course at a level of meaningful understanding, which is both a personal and a public thing. I give them *A*'s or *B*'s, which really have meaning only to those who participated in the experience, and it is a highly subjective, idiosyncratic, arbitrary judgment (HS).

[Response 3]
Grading and evaluation can be different. Grading is for assigning data for records (HS).

[Response 4]
Grades are for products and work completed. They do not necessarily reflect process and genuine learning (HS).

Question 11: "Do you observe, monitor, and assess your own teaching and learning? When? How?"

Instructional Approach 1 Response

This question was often misunderstood or left blank. For example, consider the teacher who answered: "After—during each assignment—see how successful student was" (M).

Many teachers simply did not know what we meant by this question and interpreted the phrase "assess your own teaching" to mean "feedback for students or from administrators."

Instructional Approach 2 Responses

Teachers thinking at the Instructional Approach 2 level are intent on presenting the best lessons possible and seek feedback both from students and others. These are obviously conscientious teachers but still committed to the delivery mode. What is missing is deeper self-reference in the form of self-reflection. Teachers still assume that there is a right answer or one right way to do a specific task or lesson. Here are examples:

[Response 1]
I constantly observe, assess, and monitor my teaching. When presenting a lesson, I question student understanding and alter how I present as I go along. I change methods period to period, based on students' success or frustration with assignments. I ask for feedback from students and their ideas of how to make a lesson better. When we have completed a unit, I go back over in my mind and by looking at student work for new ways of improving and write them down for the future. I share my ideas and frustrations with other team members and solicit their ideas (M).

[Response 2]
I reflect on my teaching as I teach and make modifications as I proceed through each period. I regularly assess my choice of examples and attempt to read the faces of my students and reflect upon the type of responses and questions that I get from my students (HS).

Instructional Approach 3 Responses

Instructional Approach 3 thinkers see themselves as "real-time" learners. Their teaching is almost instinctively done in the constructivist mode. When children are creating their own meanings and organizing how they want to go about learning something, then the teacher needs to get out of the way. Good Instructional Approach 3 teachers do not just work from a precise lesson plan spelled out ahead of time. They constantly monitor the total flow of the community and adjust, adapt, enhance, challenge, and add enrichment wherever and whenever appropriate. They have to be extremely flexible.

To make these adjustments, teachers constantly engage in self-reflection during the teaching itself. Only teachers capable of observing themselves in action and changing course on the basis of their own assessment of a situation can really respond to genuine student-teacher dynamic interactions. At the same time that they are observing what a student is learning, they are aware of how they are responding. They have mindfulness (Langer 1989) and what David Perkins (1995) calls reflective intelligence. These characteristics are seen in teacher responses. Response 1 is from the questionnaire; Responses 2 and 3 are interviews:

[Response 1]
As the teacher, I am also an active learner, and I complete assignments along with the students. The emotional investment in preparing to present my own perceptions to the class keeps me in touch with how the students are feeling (E).

[Response 2]
Q. Is this something anyone can walk into the classroom and start doing tomorrow? Or is it something that takes a lot of planning and training and preparing for?
A. I think BBL [brain-based learning], learning about BBL, is a process. You begin by taking baby steps. You begin looking to see what it is. And you think you know it. And as it begins to go along and you begin trying things, you realize, "I didn't really know that at all." It grows. You begin to see it from different angles. I don't think it is something that someone would just go into the classroom and say, "Oh, okay, I'm going to do BBL and I know all about it now."

But it is something that you have to go in there, and you have to start trying it because if you just try to read about it—it's not the same thing. It's something that has to be lived. You have to experience it. And as you do, you begin to realize that, yeah, your students are learning, but you're learning, too. And it's changing you. It's changing your perceptions, the way you do things, the way you think of things. And a really neat experience to have is as that's happening in the classroom, you're beginning to realize your students are really teaching you. You're teaching them, but they're teaching you, too (E).

[Response 3]
Q. When you are giving so many choices and letting the kids take so much control of the class how do you, as a teacher, keep control?
A. Well, it's a choice within parameters. I guide their choices. If it's something that's not realistic or something that we can't do, then we sit down and talk about what we could do instead.

There's one little boy right now that wants to build a dinosaur. Because we're building 16-foot whales, he now wants to build a dinosaur. I said, "Well, you know we're kind of doing the ocean, and we're doing things under the ocean and dinosaurs really weren't in the ocean."

He said, "Well, I watched the Discovery Channel the other day, and they said that dinosaurs were under the water and they had flippers and they lived in the kelp."

And I said, "Well, you go write up a plan and we'll talk about it."

And he came back to me today with the plan. He had drawn the dinosaur and the kelp. So, it's real difficult, but you still have to guide it. He will be making a dinosaur and probably, what I foresee happening, is that once he makes a dinosaur, our class will head out of the ocean and probably into dinosaurs because all kids love dinosaurs. And even though I don't want to do dinosaurs, I'll have to let that happen (Videotaped Interview with Teacher from Dry Creek Elementary School).

84

Question 13: "Teaching linked to real-life experiences can have an open-ended quality because there is no one correct answer. How can teachers teach this way without feeling a loss of control over students and what they need to learn?"

This turned out to be a throw-away question because Instructional Approach 1 and 2 teachers did not really understand it. Upon further review, however, the general lack of response from Perceptual Orientation 1 and 2 teachers (they left this one blank) suggested to us that we were getting a clearer sense of the perceptual differences between teachers since we did get Instructional Approach 3 responses:

[Response 1]
Maintaining an atmosphere of openness while maintaining discipline should not be a threat to teachers. Science constantly asks us to question the world we live in. As a teacher, one has to take chances and give students the room they need to explore. This isn't always easy (M).

[Response 2]
Class sizes, 7th grade hormones always challenge me, yet I would be an unhappy and unfulfilled teacher if I kept my teaching style too rigid. Teachers must learn to take chances and learn from failures and successes, without fear of reprisal from administrators. I believe we should be encouraged and supported to have an open-ended quality in our classroom. Flexible scheduling, administrators that encourage teachers to move away from traditional teaching, better communication or sharing between teachers, and time to share ideas and offer support are important (M).

[Response 3]
Managing real-life lessons? I don't exactly get this question. I mean there must be something wrong if learning is not linked to the natural, open-ended experiences that make up real life. How could it happen that such a schism between the real world and the world of the classroom could develop, unless no concern existed for the welfare of the children? Perhaps a key concern in education need not be control, but freedom in exploration, with the teacher as a wise and helpful companion in that pursuit (E).

We conclude with this question because the responses so beautifully illustrate the spirit of what we found. The teachers are clearly comfortable with, and welcome, freedom and openness. They equally clearly, however, respect rigor and quality. Although they may not be familiar with Deming (see, for example, Aguayo 1990), total quality control, or the theory of complex adaptive systems, they firmly believe that the process they use will more than overcome any loss of control.

What We Found: Perceptual Orientations

In the process of observing, listening, interviewing, and questioning Instructional Approach 3 teachers, we concluded that they think in fundamentally different ways from Instructional Approach 1 teachers. This new way of thinking derives from both their outlook on their job and on their larger view of the nature of reality. The consequence is that their understanding, assumptions, and beliefs create a different kind of environment, rich for student learning.

We wanted to understand these differences and give them a voice. We knew that genuinely deep change was both necessary and extremely difficult, and we felt that it could be facilitated once we had a better idea of what was actually changing. Thus, we sifted through the responses, looking for underlying patterns, and then examined these patterns further through observation and interviews.

Others have made similar attempts. John Miller (1993), for instance, has explored what he calls "orientations to curriculum which involves a basic stance to teaching and learning." The three "positions" (as he calls them) represent transmission, transaction, and transformation. Transmission is what teachers do when they conceive of the universe in "small reducible units"; transactions are what they engage in when the universe is seen as rational and intelligible, and the (traditional) scientific method prevails; and transformation follows when the universe is seen as an interconnected whole.

We endorse these positions because they capture what we found. Our research helps us identify and map more specific relationships between the instructional approaches and the larger perceptual realities of teachers. These perceptual realities are at the heart of what we now call the perceptual orientations.

The major difference is between Perceptual Orientation 1 and Perceptual Orientation 3. Perceptual Orientation 2 is transitional, representing the interim but essential path that education has to travel. In a world that is swimming in complexity, however, we believe that Perceptual Orientation 3 must be our ultimate destination. There is a difference between preparing students for a relatively stable world of agreed-upon meanings and preparing them for an intrinsically dynamical Information Age. In the latter, individual purposes and goals interact with changing contexts to drive the organization of information and the construction of meaning. It also seems to us that this type of teaching is most compatible with the communications age already upon us. Perceptual Orientation 3 thinkers are more likely to see the possibilities inherent in technology and can integrate it with a life and work filled with meaning and purpose.

Four Dimensions of Perception

Four qualities or dimensions are core elements of the perceptual orientations. These dimensions can help us grasp the differences in perception that govern the ability to implement and understand the different instructional approaches.

From Power over Others to Self-Efficacy Grounded in Authenticity

Perceptual Orientation 3 thinkers have moved from perceiving power as primarily coming from outside themselves to possessing self-efficacy, where power and decision making reside predominantly within themselves. They have developed a more solid sense of identity and believe they can affect change. Perceptual Orientation 3 teachers tend to be quite creative. Their actions are grounded in authenticity, meaning they are comfortable with self-disclosure. The espoused model and mental model become one or are closely aligned.

Expanded Cognitive Horizons

Because Perceptual Orientation 3 thinkers have a broader picture, they can deal with more complex content. Differences between facts, concepts, and the different levels of meaning are clear. Expertise is in at least one discipline or domain, and they have a felt meaning for additional disciplines. Process is important. Their sense of wholeness and interconnectedness enables them to see more connections among and between subjects, disciplines, and life.

Self-Reference and Process

Perceptual Orientation 3 teachers can engage in self-reflection and understand mindfulness; they possess reflective intelligence. Knowing the right answer is secondary; knowing how to turn a question around so that students see finding answers as their responsibility is important. They believe they are lifelong learners—awake to each moment and, in our terms, at home on the edge of possibility.

From Control to Building Relationships That Facilitate Self-Organization

Perceptual Orientation 3 teachers understand the relationships between information and experience, between learning and context, and between students and teacher. Such comprehension means they know the importance of self-organization, so they work with students to establish orderly processes, routines, and procedures. Discipline is a secondary concern because learning is organized around meaningful projects and activities. Student responsibilities range from keeping an orderly classroom and school, to helping others evaluate their work, to challenging each other.

Perceptual Orientation 2: A Transition

Our experience suggests that the primary thrust of most reform and restructuring has been to get beyond Perceptual Orientation 1 constraints. For example, behind site-based management is the idea of empowering educators, at least at the administrative level. Behind the charter schools effort is the realization that teachers must have more autonomy to select curriculum and instruction. Behind the national standards movement is a sense that educators need to be aiming higher intellectually. Behind an integrated curriculum and cooperative learning is the awareness that neither people nor content is separate. And behind the notion of authentic experience and authentic assessment is a belief that real understanding and knowledge are only possible when content is related to life.

The problem is that individuals construe and use innovations according to their mental models. And those mental models are driven by the orientation that a person has to underlying features of reality, such as the nature of power and control. Our challenge, therefore, is to work with educators at their level of perception. As that level changes, their capacities to adopt the different instructional approaches also change. Figure 5.2 shows the relationships between the instructional approaches and the perceptual orientations.

FIGURE 5.2
RELATIONSHIPS AMONG THE INSTRUCTIONAL APPROACHES
AND PERCEPTUAL ORIENTATIONS

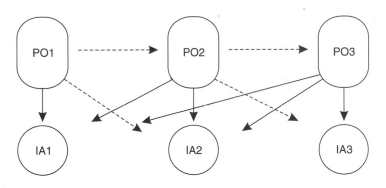

Notes
"PO" stands for Perceptual Orientation. For example, "PO1" refers to
     Perceptual Orientation 1.
"IA" stands for Instructional Approach. For example, "IA1" refers to
     Instructional Approach 1.
The dashed-line arrows represent the paths of growth.

Perceptual Orientation 3 thinkers can use all three instructional approaches. They can do what looks like Instructional Approaches 1 and 2, but the approaches are always embedded in a larger frame of reference that empowers and challenges students to do their own learning and assessment.

Getting There from Here

Perceptual Orientation 3 thinking is the heart of brain-based learning and permits the teaching that takes place on the edge of possibility. As Doris Lombard says, there is a clash between what society says and what society wants:

> We strive to nurture world-class students, individuals with the wisdom to lead humanity into the challenges of the future, by regimenting their movements in box-like enclosures we call classrooms, from which they have a limited view of the real world. I must do what I can to ensure links to the real world (Elementary School Teacher, Idyllwild School).

As people move toward Perceptual Orientation 3, their espoused models and mental models become congruent, their actions become more authentic, and their teaching becomes sophisticated enough to generate the learning that we desire in students. We need to get from here to there.

Our next step, therefore, will be to explore the characteristics of the three perceptual orientations in greater detail.

We reiterate our belief that teachers can initiate deep personal changes by changing practice and by thinking about practice in a new way. No lasting effect, however, will result unless teachers are involved in a long-term, collaborative, and intellectually challenging process that allows them to question their traditional beliefs and assumptions while they are engaged in practice. If such change on a broad scale is to happen, the system must allow for such a process.

6

From Power over Others to Self-Efficacy Grounded in Authenticity

Power: Power denotes the inherent ability or the admitted right to rule, govern, determine, etc.; authority refers to the power, because of rank or office, to give commands, enforce obedience, make decisions, etc. (the authority of a teacher).

—*Webster's New World Dictionary of the American Language* 1960

It is widely believed that intrinsically motivated, self-directed learning is the ideal model for education. Proponents of this view . . . suggest that when students learn out of curiosity and the desire for challenge, they are more involved in and satisfied with the learning, and they understand and can integrate the material more fully.

—Deci, Schwartz, Sheinman, and Ryan 1981, p. 645

The Source of Power to Act

Our observations and interviews led us to believe that one major difference between Perceptual Orientation 1 and Perceptual Orientation 3 thinkers is that the former derive most of their power from the system in which they work. They rely largely on others' authority and on their position to make learning happen in line with the mandated curriculum:

> I organize my ideas for teaching into broad thematic units. These units last six weeks or so. For example, the unit we are working on now is Celebrating Diversity. Under this umbrella, I plan activities to meet the, educational goals (in several disciplines), which have been set for my students. . . . I don't think it is feasible for a 3rd grade student to guide his own learning (Teacher).

In contrast, Perceptual Orientation 3 thinkers find their power largely in themselves. Their internalized sense of authority and belief in their own agency give them the capacity to rely primarily on their judgment based upon observations. They exercise personal autonomy.

Although both have power, what they do in the classroom is different. Perceptual Orientation 3 thinkers tend to express more belief in their own thinking and ideas; Perceptual Orientation 1 thinkers depend more directly on prescribed procedure or the correct answer. We identified this internal quality as self-efficacy.

Self-efficacy is the "exercise of personal agency" (Bandura 1992). It focuses on an individual's belief of who is in charge and makes things happen. In our view, self-efficacy is the alternative to downshifting.

Self-efficacy is important for two reasons. First, it frees educators from many of the system's perceived constraints, enabling them to introduce new ideas, methods, and approaches, with or without the support of the system. Perceptual Orientation 3 thinkers seem to handle change better because they can suspend judgment more readily. In Ellen Langer's terms (1989), they have fewer "category traps," more or less rigid beliefs that guide what they do in their moment-to-moment encounters with the dynamic world of the classroom and life. Second, in general, to elicit self-efficacy in students takes a teacher with self-efficacy:

> Teachers who [were] more autonomy oriented [had] children who are more intrinsically motivated. . . . [and] children in their classes

[had] higher self-esteem—they felt better about themselves in general and they perceived themselves to be more competent in the cognitive domain—the domain that relates directly to the classroom (Deci et al. 1981, p. 647).

The problem is that the education system has institutionalized a way of thinking based on the power of position, rather than on personal power or the self-efficacy of its participants. Educators have power by virtue of their position in the educational hierarchy and the sanctions that are vested in that position. Most educators have been trained in or molded to this way of thinking, as have many people in the community—at least when they think about education. Perceptual Orientation 3 thinkers have taken issue with the belief that the system defines the scope of their capacity to decide and act.

We should add that a particular quality of self-efficacy is important to us. A belief in one's own capacity to take charge can result in an abuse of power, such as acting like a tyrant. That is not the quality we observed. Rather, we saw self-efficacy grounded in authenticity. The difference between the two types is reflected in how much people "walk their talk." What we saw in Perceptual Orientation 3 thinkers was that their espoused theory (what they said) was congruent with their mental model (the beliefs that actually drove their actions).

This chapter describes the differences between dependency on the system and self-efficacy and then looks in more detail at how the differences play themselves out in education and in the educators with whom we worked.

The Education System as a Power Hierarchy

Layers are pervasive in nature. Everything comes in layers—even the human brain is organized in layers to some extent (see Paul MacLean's theory of the triune brain in *Making Connections* [Caine and Caine 1994a]). A generic term to describe some aspects of this layering of an organization is hierarchy.

The social organization of most species is hierarchical, with a dominant male or female. In Darwinist terms, this arrangement means that a species as a whole will survive because the most powerful genes are favored. The consequence, however, is a pecking order. The weakest members of a flock, herd, or tribe are continually weakened because they get the least; the strongest members are continually strengthened because the power of their position ensures they get the most.

Historically, the education system was set up to model a command-and-control hierarchy, which was used as far back as the Chinese and Romans to maintain and administer their empires. Morris (1995) suggests that hierarchies were employed in the United States and elsewhere by industrial developers such as John D. Rockefeller to administer their factories and business empires. One good reason for adopting this mode of organization is that it led to stability and ease of control because people were given precise roles and functions. Thus, the model for education reflected the model employed throughout the world of business and government.

The practical result is that people derive their power and authority from the position they hold in the system, and they use that power to sustain the system by specifying and carrying out responsibilities and activities that these positions define. By functioning in this way, however, the system itself interferes with the capacity to grow, learn, evolve, and adapt to a changing world. Richard Pascale (1990) highlights this dilemma:

> In evolution, [the saying] "nothing fails like success" is probably always right. A creature which has become perfectly adapted to its environment, an animal whose whole capacity and vital force is concentrated and expanded in succeeding here and now, has nothing left over with which to respond to any radical change. Age by age, it becomes more perfectly economical in the way its entire resources meet exactly its current and customary opportunities. In the end, it can do all that is necessary to survive without any conscious striving or unadapted movement. It can, therefore, beat all competitors in the special field; but equally, should the field change, it must become extinct (p. 15).

A Hidden Contradiction for Education

This dilemma—maintaining a hierarchy that inhibits growth while purporting to seek growth—exposes a contradiction between what education says it does or intends to do and the mental model that influences what its moment-to-moment actions are based upon. In other words, the system itself lacks authenticity. Education purports to be an actualization hierarchy (Eisler 1987). In such a hierarchy, "the function is to maximize the organism's potential" (Wilber 1995, p. 23). The system works in the service of the people engaged in it, offering opportunities and support for all members to become more of what they can be.

But schools and the educational system are based on a command-and-control structure. Rather than actualization hierarchies, they are what Eisler refers to as domination hierarchies. They are hierarchies "based on force or the express or implied threat of force" (Wilber 1995, p. 22). Rather than the system serving people, people serve the system. Often, the consequence is that those lower down in the pecking order are the most controlled and contained, not the most facilitated. People are kept in their place, and many lose the capacity to function at the higher levels, efforts that are supposedly encouraged. We should add that this model, and the contradiction inherent in it, also pervade society at large.

Downshifting as a Consequence of Exercising Power

As we point out (see Caine and Caine 1997), people downshift when they feel helpless. They revert to early programming or instinctive behaviors and lose much of their capacity to think creatively and tolerate risk, uncertainty, and ambiguity. In effect, they experience the opposite of self-efficacy. By using power based almost exclusively on a command-and-control structure, educators induce helplessness and compliance, activate early programming, and reduce the willingness and ability of education and students to take personal risks. Such risks are the hallmark of the exploration that accompanies genuine intellectual struggles.

For adults employed by the system, the rewards and punishment are job security and money. For students, they are grades and, ultimately, credentials. Such an approach discourages risk-taking:

> What rewards and punishments do is induce compliance, and this they do very well indeed. If your objective is to get people to obey an order, to show up on time, and do what they're told, then bribing or threatening them may be sensible strategies (Kohn 1993, p. 41).

Our research and related evidence (see Caine and Caine 1994a) suggest that when the teacher uses power to force learning, when the students comply with the demands because they will receive rewards (whether grades or favorable treatment), and when such learning is independent of meaning, personal goals, or purposes, then students will downshift to some degree. As Alfie Kohn points out:

> But if your objective is to get long-term quality in the workplace, to help students become careful thinkers and self-directed learners, or to support children in developing good values, then rewards, like punishments, are absolutely useless. In fact, as we are beginning to see, they are worse than useless—they are actually counterproductive (Kohn 1993, pp. 41, 42).

We maintain that if educators want students to learn meaningfully, then they have to provide different conditions. In particular, they have to understand how the overt and subliminal use of power affects students. When a teacher uses power to induce students to do what they are told, and when it is combined with lack of meaning and purpose and a passive "going along" with what students are asked to do, then such students are not in a low threat/high challenge mode, and genuine complex learning will not take place:

> When we are working for a reward, we do exactly what is necessary to get it and no more. Not only are we less apt to notice peripheral features of the task, but in performing it we are also less likely to take chances, play with possibilities, follow hunches that might not pay off. Risks are to be avoided whenever possible

because the objective is not to engage in an open-ended encounter with ideas; it is simply to get the goody. One group of researchers explained that when we are motivated by rewards, "features such as predictability and simplicity are desirable, since the primary focus associated with this orientation is to get through the task expediently in order to reach the desired goal." Another psychologist was more succinct: rewards, he said are the "enemies of exploration" (Kohn 1993, p. 63).

An education system that employs power and induces downshifting therefore prevents maximum learning. It restricts one's perspective, reflection, creative thinking, and ability to live with paradox and engage in most forms of higher-order thinking. When educators downshift learners, they generate "programming" through data input in much the way people can program a computer. In general, therefore, the current education system grossly underutilizes the ability of the human brain to learn.

How the Power of the System Is Played Out in the Lives of Its Members

To see what we have been discussing more clearly, let's observe some students, teachers, and administrators.

The World Called School: The Students' World

Observing teachers and examining their responses to questions and interviews convinced us that teachers had varying degrees of commitment to power and authority. As described in Chapters 4 and 5, we began our observations by looking at the conditions for learning that most of our teachers had provided in their classes. Needless to say, the classes resembled the downshifted conditions. What intrigued us was the agreed-upon belief that these conditions were a necessity. Although these teachers were intelligent professionals with knowledge and disciplinary expertise, they had mental models of learning and teaching that defined learning as the product produced when the downshifted conditions were correctly imposed. We saw how critical the totality of the environment was in influencing thinking and practice.

Here is a scenario: As we walk into the classroom, a teacher is telling some students that they have to do a specific task (e.g., read a book, do problems, or finish an experiment) by this Friday, when they will have a test. The teacher encourages the students to practice and do whatever it takes to do well on the test. The test will result in a grade. The test grade will determine their overall grade, and the implication is that all sorts of bad consequences come from bad grades.

What is important to understand is that the teacher is the accepted authority. The teacher is the one with the power to provide a grade based upon accomplishing a specific task or product, regardless of whether that task has any meaning. When the teacher sets time limits, specifies exactly what students have to do, and ignores the reality that what is being learned is almost totally meaningless, fragmented, and motivated only by the fear of grades, teachers have downshifted students. Most students will do exactly what is required but will remain passive. The thinking that goes beyond basic demands will be short circuited. In a sense, students feel helpless to do anything except what the teacher asks.

The problem is that while students are in this state, which reflects their momentary reality, they will not take the time to understand why they are learning or, more correctly, why they are doing what they are doing. We tested this theory by going around to students in numerous schools and classes where Instructional Approach 1 was evident and asking them why they were doing what the teacher had assigned. We found no students who could articulate a purpose for what they were doing other than something related to punishment. In the lower grades, sample answers included, "If I don't do it, I have to stay in for recess"; in the upper grades, "I don't know" or "I need the grade." Students also could not relate what they were learning to a personal goal or see connections between their assignment and the world outside of school. Complex associations to other fields of study were inevitably absent, as well as the ability to question or challenge a topic or parts of a topic.

The Teacher's World

But what about the conditions for the teacher? Do teachers take time to reflect? To do complex thinking? To generate creative solutions and engage in intellectual discussions? The answer turned out to be a resounding no. One reason is that in almost 100 percent of U.S. public schools, there is little time between classes, plus little time dedicated to teacher reflection, to genuine teacher dialogue. So time, or lack of it, as teachers and students move from one class to the next, inhibits complex learning and change.

If we begin to look at the forces that dominate in a school, then we see that the teachers are in much the same boat as the students:

> The present study suggests that when teachers feel pressured by superiors, they tend to become more controlling with their students. Further, one of the things that appears to make teachers feel pressured and therefore become more controlling is having it emphasized that they are responsible for their students' performing up to standards. When this occurs, teachers tend to lecture and explain more, and they give children less choice and less opportunity for autonomous learning (Deci, Spiegel, Ryan, Koestner, and Kauffman 1982, p. 858).

When students are told what to study, without having any input, and teachers are told what the curriculum is, both are experiencing compliance and helplessness. When students are told what to learn by what deadline, they share with teachers the experience that comes with being told what they have to teach, what they have to cover by this time, and when the grades are due. Students may be afraid of getting a bad grade, but teachers share similar fears. All we need to do is challenge a teacher on the grade given a student—woe to the teacher who cannot justify grades based on an accurate accounting of meaningless points. Given these conditions, teachers have little opportunity to reflect, ask why or how a procedure is relevant, or figure out how a task is relevant to how students learn. As we studied the conditions that supported the way teachers taught, we began to have a clearer understanding of the deeper layers and assumptions that operate not only in the school but also throughout the educational system and society.

The Administrator's World

And what of superintendents? Surely they are free to invent, plan, and use creative solutions and higher-order complex thinking and planning to create better school systems. Our observations show the opposite. Perhaps the most telling experience occurred in a workshop with superintendents. In the middle of our workshop, we were shunted aside by the state superintendent's aide, who informed us that the state superintendent had important information to divulge and needed time alone with our workshop participants. The most intriguing part of the experience was the aura of power surrounding this particular superintendent. This state superintendent was by all appearances a political animal, something that was amply confirmed by the superintendents in our workshop.

We went to the hotel restaurant and waited for the session to end. When we reappeared in the room, we found a group of angry and devastated people. Apparently they had received their "report cards"—how well their districts had scored on the state exams. They were convinced that the districts with low scores would see heads roll. They fully understood what we meant by downshifting. Here is a comment from an administrator who is at Perceptual Orientation 3:

> I thought for years that I was so out of place as an administrator that I should leave the profession. If something even marginally promising had come along, I would have [originally]. I felt that all administrators were my colleagues, even the superintendent, that teachers were the heart of the profession, and we needed to revise our processes and roles so that teachers felt themselves to be the heart. They could then carry that feeling to the children they taught.
>
> Political survival is the milieu [of] the reality I worked in, even at the building level. I despaired. What was even worse, the teachers' association fed into and off of this political process, and reinforced the teacher's sense of powerlessness as a means to create its own

political base and political survival. Paternalism and pats on the head are as close as I can come to describing the system's approach to the teaching staff. And the teachers' association and the district administrators have the collusion going that bickering over money is what is important to these teachers.

I still feel out of place, as if I don't belong. I've quit caring about that. I just do what I can to make this system work for teachers and for kids, put up a good show (dress like an administrator at the proper time, hand in the appropriate reports, appear deferent at the appropriate times), and care fiercely about keeping this system from doing any more damage, in part by teaching kids how to cope with milestones that grind exceedingly fine.

Throughout the system, the exercise of power over others and deference to power are prevalent and have a devastating effect. They create dependence and compliance and reduce risk-taking and genuine questioning and honesty. They isolate individuals and lead to alienation among constituents and blame and competition rather than cooperation. The use of power and the resultant sense of helplessness contribute to passive-aggressive behavior all too evident for anyone spending time in teachers' lounges. The fear engendered also breeds a dependence on rules and bureaucracy and limits genuine learning and innovation.

Another Hidden Contradiction

Few within the system see that what they do to others is being done to them. It is as if everyone is caught up in an invisible web and has never taken the opportunity to see if things could be changed:

It is easy for a teacher to object to a program of merit pay—to see how patronizing it is to be bribed with extra money for doing what some administrator decides is a good job. It takes more effort for the teacher to see how the very same is true of grades or offers of extra recess when she becomes the controller. Exactly the same is true of the worker, chafing under the burden of a manipulative compensation plan, who comes home and manipulates his child with a Skinnerian system that differs only in the type of reward (Kohn 1993, p. 28).

The Alternative: Self-Efficacy Grounded in Authenticity

As noted earlier, self-efficacy is the "exercise of personal agency" (Bandura 1992). Bandura calls self-efficacy a

> "self-referent phenomenon" in the sense that it happens automatically and spontaneously within an individual and is largely independent of pressure from someone or something outside of the individual. Instead of wondering how to fulfill someone else's need or desire, individuals with high self-efficacy appear to search out their own thinking and respond accordingly. It is their own beliefs, thoughts, and moral or ethical fiber that gives meaning and value to external events (Bandura 1992).

Studies have shown that individuals with high self-efficacy tend to have common characteristics:

- Set higher goals and believe that they will succeed.
- Visualize success. Those with low self-efficacy tend to visualize failure.
- Possess better skills to manage emotional reactions that can improve the quality of thinking and action, and can use such skills under taxing conditions.
- Perform better, regardless of ability.
- Discover more quickly what strategies work.
- Work harder.
- Possess a more positive attitude.

We interpret such research to mean that these individuals are resilient to conditions that lead to downshifting. Bandura (1992) concludes that "it requires self-efficacy to remain task oriented in the face of pressing situational demands and situations which have social repercussions."

As we observed educators, they began to reveal an additional quality that emerges in many different spheres of human behavior. In the words of Art Combs, some educators were becoming adequate persons:

> The need for each person is for adequacy. The development of a richer, broader, more fluid field means seeking new experience and new perceptions, confronting belief with belief, even placing oneself in predicaments for the risky job of finding one's own best way. . . . It calls for increasingly accepting oneself while recognizing one's failures and inadequacies. Such a quest is not easy, for it requires placing oneself in jeopardy. This kind of risking or flirting with inadequacy requires courage and determination, the encouragement of significant others, and even willingness to put oneself in the position of being hurt (Combs, Richards, and Richards 1988, p. 294).

The notion of adequacy was important because the definition includes the capacity to see more options, the tendency to test and revise actions, and the ability to predict the outcome of one's actions. Adequate persons are open to experience (Rogers 1969). A definition of adequacy also includes an enhanced capacity to deal more effectively with ambiguities and uncertainties:

> Adequate personalities do not need to have an immediate answer to problems. . . . They are able to live comfortably with an unsolved problem. Consequently, they are less likely to accept partial solutions to problems as sufficient or final (Combs et al. 1988, p. 271).

Because their sense of self does not depend on the opinion of others, adequate persons feel united with others. They are "democratic people in the deepest possible sense" (Maslow, in Combs et al. 1988, p. 276). Adequate persons

> have much concern for other people, which shows itself in humanitarian interests and in close association with some of our great attempts at social welfare. They are often motivated by love, understanding, and compassion. . . . They do not find it necessary

103

to use others for solely personal gratification and, as a consequence, can develop themselves more fully to other people. They have the capacity to "give of themselves" (Combs et al. 1988, pp. 275–276).

The characteristics of self-efficacy are the qualities that students need to survive in the technologically rich future. They need to be self-starting and self-directed learners. They need to be able to persist with their own thinking in the face of pressure to conform. They need to believe in themselves and in their abilities to master difficult material and solve complex problems. In short, they need to be empowered.

It is up to the teachers, then, to empower students. And people with self-efficacy tend to more naturally elicit self-efficacy in others:

> The more effective person has a broader concept of self, which is by no means restricted to his personal being, but which is also concerned with the welfare of others. As a consequence, what he does to achieve personal adequacy contributes also to the adequacy of society (Combs et al. 1988, p. 60).

Servant Leadership as a Model

Because of our obsessions with how leaders behave and with the interactions of leaders and followers, we forget that in essence, leadership is about learning how to shape the future. Leadership exists when people are no longer victims of circumstances but participate in creating new circumstances. When people operate in this domain of generative leadership, day by day, they come to a deepening understanding of . . ."how the universe actually works." That is the real gift of leadership. It's not about positional power; it's not about accomplishments; it's ultimately not even about what we do. Leadership is about creating a domain in which human beings continually deepen their understanding of reality and become more capable of participating in the unfolding of the world. Ultimately, leadership is about creating new realities.

—Senge 1996, p. 3

Historically, leadership has been regarded as the action of someone out in front or at the top of the hierarchy guiding us in our actions and showing and telling us what to do. While there is still an element of truth in this understanding, leadership is now being dramatically reframed. As we begin to grasp a reality in which everything is defined by its relationship to everything else, the relationship between the leader and the led is also being defined.

The characteristics of leadership described by humanists 50 years ago are being resurrected in much of the more recent work on the nature of leadership. One of those characteristics is self-efficacy. Another is service.

Robert Greenleaf coined the term "servant leadership" in 1970. He believed that leadership should begin with a natural feeling for service. That desire to serve includes both serving others and serving a higher purpose. There is a reappraisal of the value of and appreciation for those who are led. Such leadership has far-reaching benefits:

> At its core, servant leadership is a long-term, transformational approach to life and work, in essence, a way of being that has the potential to create positive change throughout our society (Spears 1995, p. 4).

In our terms, a servant-leader has self-efficacy grounded in authenticity. This quality is accompanied by a sense of responsibility both for living the principles that are espoused, in public and in private, and for creating the opportunities for others to live authentic lives.

Differences Among the Perceptual Orientations

As we mentioned at the beginning of the chapter, one profound difference between Perceptual Orientation 1 and 3 thinkers is their source of power. The former derive power from the system; the latter find power in themselves. Here we contrast the two and then describe Perceptual Orientation 2 as a state of transition.

Perceptual Orientation 1

Perceptual Orientation 1 teachers are largely outer directed, relying on others' authority. They measure success by praise and approval gleaned from others.

A Sense of Self That Depends on an Artificial Ideal

Change is often difficult because it challenges how people define themselves. As we observed our teachers moving along the perceptual orientations, we often witnessed a painful breaking with comfort zones:

> Part of my fear is that I can't control the pace—I have always thought of myself as a one of the "good" teachers—dedicated and willing to do what's best for my students. I have a reputation for successfully dealing with the students other teachers have given up on. What if, during all these changes, I fall behind? What if I can't do it and fall behind? What if I can't stay up with the "good" teachers in this paradigm shift? There goes my sense of self (Teacher).

Deference to the System

Perceptual Orientation 1 and to some extent Perceptual Orientation 2 thinkers defer to the system, even when they are critical of specific individuals or decisions. They view learning and performance as replications or creations of what an authority has prescribed. Their thinking goes something like this: "As a teacher, my job is determined by individuals and institutions with the appropriate power and knowledge, and because of this the materials—the curriculum and the mandates—are basically good."

Teachers, and we include administrators and some college professors, with Perceptual Orientation 1 thinking rarely question the power inherent in the system. In one university, for instance, we observed responses to the administration's questioning grade inflation that some professors of education had used. Even though the professors were angry, they believed that they needed to search out ways to accommodate such questioning. They did not see it as their job to question the thinking behind the administrators' concern, even though they supposedly had the expertise to defend grading practices in their courses.

106

When one person did question why the faculty's practices were not adequately respected or why they, as researchers and lecturers on grading policy, were not seen as the definers of how grading should be done, that person's remarks were met with collective silence and ultimately ignored. In general, Perceptual Orientation 1 thinkers tend not to challenge authority or "rock the boat."

A Demand for Authority over Those Below—the Students

In a physics class, a student worn thin with disenchantment burst out with, "What has this ___ got to do with my life?" The teacher looked momentarily bewildered and confused. After all, who had the right to speak to her in such a fashion? Such vulgarity, such arrogance, such ignorance. Her authority was in question. In an instant, the steel came back into the teacher's delivery and with all the Newtonian principles of force and action, the student was impaled. The teacher spate her answer at the student: "I couldn't expect that you were in any way capable of understanding the mind that created these equations. Nor should I expect that your little MTV-decimated brain could see anything beyond your next bout with acne." Filled with power of authority, content, and status, she pointed to the door and said, "Out—I will see you in the office when class is over."

—Samples 1995, p. 5

The same reliance on powerful others that often creates helplessness and compliance in teachers is actually a value that most teachers have internalized. Teachers think that having power over students with evaluations and grades is appropriate. This faith in power is also the basis for believing that people have to be made to do things that are good for them. Such thinking not only justifies but also calls for the use of punishment and reward as the extrinsic motivator. Intrinsic motivation is seen only as "you should want to do this on your own" or "this is for your own good."

One might argue that what we observed was the authoritarian personality in action or perhaps a particular learning style or Kohlberg's (1981) Stage 4 (law and order). Although all three suppositions may be true, our research suggests that these teachers also behave this way because the system and their experiences have led them to behave this way. Teachers exhibit this type of behavior—one that is highly resistant to change—because they are caught in a dominance hierarchy. But they are capable of "metamorphosing" when a process helps them to question their assumptions and to take personal charge of their own thinking and evolution.

Perceptual Orientation 3

Perceptual Orientation 3 teachers buy into the educational system—after all, they are spending their lives working in it. There is a level, however, at which they are inner directed: They do not take the doctrine of the system for granted the way their Perceptual Orientation 1 colleagues do. This inner freedom reveals itself in their ability to incorporate district and administrative demands into a fluid, creative, and collaborative classroom so that such demands do not fragment meanings. It also shows itself in other ways.

An Integrated Sense of Self

Perceptual Orientation 3 thinkers have developed a strong sense of self. They are not arrogant (though they can be); rather, they are comfortable with their own view of themselves. They have an internal locus of control (Phares 1976)

Here is part of an interview between one of us (Geoffrey) and a high school teacher:

> **Teacher:** As you will see, the only thing that limits us is our own definition of what we're supposed to be teaching by the course title of the discipline we're working in.

> **Geoffrey:** Okay. You actually feel a great deal of that autonomy?

> **Teacher:** I feel that completely—outrageously so. . . . So if I'm looking at, "What can I do in my classroom," it's pretty much anything that I want. Now this gets—later on—I don't want it to sound like, "Yes, I'll do whatever I want to do." No. There are some moral constraints, also institutional constraints that exist.

A Willingness to Open Up and Question the System

Perceptual Orientation 3 thinkers question the system. They are willing to explore and examine ideas that the system either keeps separate or ignores. As one administrator said to us: "It never ceases to amaze me how many teachers ask permission to do things which should never need another's approval."

An Ability to Generate Self-Efficacy in Students

Perceptual Orientation 3 thinkers act as a buffer between their students and those aspects of the system that lead to downshifting. They can engage their students, acknowledge student interests, challenge them, and generally so empower the students that students are willing to take risks and work on more complex and demanding levels. Several teacher comments exemplify this ability:

> [Comment 1]
> Student leaders provide another step toward independence, and thus empowerment. Toward the end of the second week or two, we discuss the possibilities various disasters might present, among them a disabling injury to myself:
>
> "In such a case, look around the room carefully to see whom you would most trust to use good judgment and take over the leadership of the class. Which three people would you choose to be fair and wise about what to do in an emergency? Please vote by writing the three names on the secret ballot."
>
> Lots of kids put their own name, that of their best friend, and a carefully made choice. The two top vote-getters become coleaders of the class and are subsequently called upon to perform various responsible functions. Leading the line for the fire drills, bringing the emergency pack, conducting a class vote for a suitable reward, posing suggestions as to the resolution of problems that confront the class from time to time, are all examples of students empowered to cope with the real world (Elementary School Teacher).

The second comment is an interview between one of us (Geoffrey) and a high school teacher:

[Comment 2]

Teacher: But the idea is if you model this kind of behavior—if people see you broadly interpreting and breaking down the boundaries among disciplines, which is what we try to do. . . . There is a question here on empowerment and that's the idea, that the kids feel empowered by this. That's our whole point. We don't want to dictate what is the cannon. There is no cannon.

Geoffrey: You're raising all sorts of issues. Let me just take one and deal with the extent to which your students feel the same sort of autonomy that you do. Do you think that they do? . . .

Teacher: We have letters and testimonies, etc., from the students. The kids then, when they leave, should no longer feel limited when they go to another course. . . . like astrophysics. They've seen it done somewhere else.

Geoffrey: Do they [the students] begin to think at those levels?

Teacher: It's amazing how they do. I wish I could bring in some of our student papers. . . . Teachers [come to visit] and when we first started this integrated course [they said], "Na, it's too hard. Kids can't do that." Well, the kids don't know that. They have no idea and they're discussing things at a level and they moan at first and groan because it's work. But [they are] at a level you would find in an [advanced] humanities course or graduate seminar without a doubt. Their responses when they go on to universities are very positive. But yes—I'm not saying they all get it. Some struggle very hard.

Geoffrey: To what extent do you invite them to challenge you? For instance, you've just said there is no cannon. That's one of the constructs that drives you. . . . To what extent are the kids invited to question your perspective?

Teacher: Okay. That's one part of the question you asked, "How do you create a low threat/high challenge area?" First of all, M— and I argue in an animated fashion in front of the [students] all the time. In fact, when we first started the course three years ago, we were going to divide it up. I would teach one day, she would teach the next day, and then we would teach together one day

110

out of the cycle. Well, the kids said, "No. We want you both here all the time." And when we first started teaching there, the arguments were much more heated because we both . . .

Geoffrey: . . . touching a genuine interest.

Teacher: A genuine interest and we're both not shy people. . . . And the kids will jump right in. . . . And also when you ask, "Do I create a low threat/high challenge?" That's another thing. I think as a student, you have some responsibility for creating a low threat/high challenge environment. . . .

Geoffrey: So you—what you're suggesting to me is that as you relax as a teacher—relaxes with themselves and with their need to control the students—they can in fact begin to challenge them at higher and higher levels and the [students] will not feel threatened.

Teacher: They shouldn't feel threatened. That's part of the learning experience—is not to feel threatened. . . . So if you are afraid of a challenge, it's part of the learning process to get past that fear (Interview with high school teacher).

Perceptual Orientation 2: A State of Transition

When it comes to the extent of self-efficacy, many educators are somewhere in the middle. Moreover, the range of this middle ground is extensive. It extends from those who are just embarking on freeing up students but still rely heavily on what the system expects them to do, to those who understand that students need to be self-directed but still use the power of their position to make sure that things are "done right." What they all do in common is to use the system for the security and support that they do not find in themselves. This approach means that they are caught in a perceptual tension that may be invisible to them. They want empowerment and to empower students and yet subscribe to a system based on beliefs that innately tend to disempower people. Here is one illustration from an elementary school teacher:

> Because I so easily downshift, I am sensitive to the negative role
> of threat in learning. I have developed systems which revolve
> about actively involved students, designed to keep us all safe and
> secure enough to be able to take the risks inherent in learning.

The point is that the teacher is aware of downshifting and of the need to protect students from feeling helpless so that students can be empowered. This awareness is particularly warranted in the early grades. At the same time, this need to protect because of one's own fear may infect, not empower, students. There is a fine line between helping children and empowering them. Perhaps the following adage (which most of us are familiar with) says it best: "Give me a fish, I'll eat for a day. Teach me to fish, I eat for a lifetime."

Here is a comment from a middle school teacher:

> I continually ask myself as I prepare lessons or during lessons,
> "What part of this could I give to my students to do?" Sometimes,
> if you watch, I start to do something as, "the teacher is in charge
> here," and suddenly realize that the students could do this, and I
> give my leadership role to them. My students lead, stretch, make
> group or individual decisions about how they want to accomplish
> a goal, sometimes set by them or they have a voice in setting my
> directions. I try to keep in mind that students have a great store
> of knowledge to share with each other and me. Students have
> given me wonderful ideas on what they want to learn next and
> how they would like to learn it. They have definite ideas on
> projects they would like to do. Instead of often asking them
> questions or giving them questions about what they have read or
> about math, I have them write the questions for each other or for
> themselves to answer!

This quote is a beautiful example of a teacher in transition to Perceptual Orientation 3 thinking. The teacher is working hard to empower students; clearly has the ability to learn from them; and is open to receiving ideas from many sources, so she is not threatened by students who may know more than she does. At the same time, the underlying frame is one in which she prepares lessons and decides what she could give her students to do. This kind of thinking indicates a still-firm, taken-for-granted belief in her power of position and in her responsibility to make learning happen.

Being on the cusp between subscribing to the system and empowering students can be an extremely uncomfortable position to occupy. These are the people for whom our change process is critical but often, at least at first, quite unsettling. The lack or availability also plays a role.

Summary of Differences in Self-Efficacy

We used indicators (see Figure 6.1 on p. 114) to guide us in assessing where a person fell on the continuum that shows the degree of self-efficacy. Each indicator represents a point on the continuum, from Perceptual Orientation 1 to Perceptual Orientation 3. We appreciate that this assessment is qualitative and that the indicators do not adequately deal with such problems as differences in context. We should add that moving along the continuum cannot be taught by direct instruction. Change occurs over time as people experience and work with appropriate processes, such as those we describe in this book and in *Mindshifts* (Caine, Caine, and Crowell 1994).

We also need to emphasize that although our primary focus is on teachers and teacher change, what we observed applies equally to the perception of administrators. Administrators with a Perceptual Orientation 1 perspective can neither understand nor appreciate Perceptual Orientation 3 teachers. Administrators concerned with power can also play havoc with genuine systemic restructuring.

Similarly, this dilemma can be extended to the community and school boards committed to schools and a system run by those in power. When they see their job as making things happen rather than as facilitating system change through self-organization, the change process becomes too turbulent, and all too often little real change can take place.

FIGURE 6.1

**INDICATORS OF SELF-EFFICACY ALONG
THE PERCEPTUAL ORIENTATIONS CONTINUUM**

The Perceptual Orientation 1 End of the Continuum	The Perceptual Orientation 3 End of the Continuum
The extent to which individuals remarked on their own powerlessness.	The extent to which individuals' language indicated a focus on their own decision making and the taking of responsibility and credit for their innovations.
The extent to which individuals worked with procedures that depended on the power of position. Examples include direct rewards, punishment, coercion, and indirect bribes.	The extent to which individuals fostered independence and independent decision making in students, so that they shared power and responsibility with students.
The extent to which individuals deferred to prescribed procedures based on the need to please an external authority.	The extent to which individuals modified directions from the system, such as grading and planning mandates.
The extent to which individuals implemented new methods, procedures, and strategies in which they had been trained, irrespective of student or class needs.	The extent to which individuals felt free to reinterpret, ignore, or modify new methods, procedures, and strategies in which they had been trained—actions based on their perceptions of student or contextual needs.
The extent to which individuals were indifferent to the real needs of others—students, colleagues, and parents.	The extent to which individuals were aware of others' needs and sought to help others satisfy their needs.
The extent to which a dissonance existed between what individuals professed and what they did, or between what they did in one setting (say, with colleagues) and in others (say, in the classroom or with parents).	The extent to which congruence existed between what individuals professed and what they did, and between their behaviors in multiple settings and contexts.

7

Expanded Cognitive Horizons

*She had a very good way of showing us that it was not just this one
thing, it was the whole thing and you had to question every piece
in it.*

—Student at Peninsula Middle School (Fadiman 1988)

One dominant theme in recent times has been a concern about
educational standards and a search for excellence. At one end of the
spectrum is the simple wish for all people to be literate. At the other
end is the desire for world-class standards that all students can achieve
from a public school education. We echo and endorse the goal of setting
higher levels of performance and understanding throughout the educational system. Our concern is that orthodox ways of thinking about
education are interfering with its march toward higher quality.

The top graduate schools in the United States demonstrate the
pursuit of excellence and are generally regarded as the best in the
world. They are populated by professionals who are masters of their
disciplines and who have high expectations for their students. Thus,
the model for teachers and students alike emphasizes such activities as
individual research, systematic thought, critical analysis, and practical
applications. We suggest that, in many respects, this model represents
the epitome of brain-based learning and that it should be available from
kindergarten on.

A second theme is notable by its absence in public discourse. Educators should be doing more than just providing an education that is limited to preparing people for jobs and "productive" participation in society. Part of education's function is to help people experience the sheer joy and privilege of learning as a way of appreciating life itself. The time has come to acknowledge that the search for understanding embraces our deepest meanings, including the spiritual, even if as a consequence of such exploration, people decide that the spiritual is an illusion. Awe and continuing mystery are core aspects of the human experience.

Ultimate purposes enliven intrinsic motivation. Large frames of reference help organize and make sense of specific domains and skills. It seems to us that by appreciating the joy of existence itself, we open ourselves and children to our potential and to the natural pursuit of excellence.

The phrase that seems the most appropriate to convey this scope of thought and awareness is "cognitive horizons." Perceptual Orientation 3 thinkers are capable of generating excellence and joy in their students, in part because they have broader cognitive horizons than do Perceptual Orientation 1 and 2 thinkers.

Definition of Cognitive Horizons

A "horizon," according to the *World Book Dictionary* (1979), is "the limit of one's thinking, experience, interest, or outlook." Such a definition summarizes one element of what we mean by cognitive horizons. The phrase refers to the range, scope, or categories of possibilities of which one can realistically conceive. Cognitive horizons also includes a dynamical element: Cognitive horizons are not permanently fixed. Dynamism means that categories can change and possibilities can be conceived in response to changing and unique contexts.

Cognitive horizons represent the limits of the "maps" people use to navigate through the world of information and meaning. The larger and more dynamical the maps, the more room they have to maneuver, and the easier they can roam without getting lost.

On Becoming a Gardener: An Allegory

We introduce our notion of broad cognitive horizons through an allegory:

> Imagine that you want to become a really good gardener. You have wandered through many beautiful gardens, thrilled by the possibilities. You finally have a place where you can grow your own garden. You want to do it well. And you would appreciate some help.

> One offer comes from a person who has read a great deal, but who has not actually created a garden you admire. You politely decline that person's offer, at least for the time being. You know other people who are clearly experts, but their assistance would be intermittent. It dawns on you that you actually want a teacher or coach.

> One day, you meet the friend of a friend. The former used to do gardening shows for TV, has a wonderful garden, and was once a teacher. You and Robin (the name we'll use) resonate and decide that you will work together. Your interest is clear. Robin looks forward to seeing the world of gardening through new eyes. It will be a partnership of discovery.

> Over time, Robin introduces you to many possibilities. You visit many gardens; prepare beds; plant seeds, bulbs, bushes and trees; read books and magazines; engage in countless discussions; are entertained (and occasionally annoyed) by butterflies, birds, and insects; figure out ways to protect your garden from dogs, children, neighbors, and pests; feel the texture of bark, leaves, and grass; delight in the fragrance of honeysuckle, roses, and herbs; and begin to recognize names and varieties.

> You also find that gardening is not always easy or enjoyable. Sometimes you have to work quickly, in bad weather. Sometimes, no matter how many different solutions you try, a plant does not grow. Sometimes you work elbow deep in mud, in humid weather, surrounded by midges, wondering what on earth it is all about.

And yet the unpleasantness wears off, the results are exciting, your interest and achievements carry you through, and you learn.

Robin knows that you cannot grasp gardening all at once. You have to try things out, see the consequences of over- and underwatering, and experience the seasons. Sometimes you and Robin visit and then discuss gardens, focusing and expanding on points of interest and constantly building your picture of what is possible.

In the course of your adventure, Robin introduces ideas and materials that initially startle you and yet add greatly to your understanding. Robin sees that you have a poster of a Monet painting of his garden at Giverny. That observation leads to a discussion on the use of light and color in Impressionist paintings, and Robin then introduces you to some real gardens designed in the manner of Impressionist art. On another occasion, you move from the design of gardens to a discussion about design generally, and you find yourselves enthusiastically comparing the design of a garden to interior decorating and to the design of a computer database. Together, you and Robin find that the very idea of design takes on a whole new set of meanings that are quite exciting. In fact, your ideas get Robin excited about the relationship between gardening and a host of new technologies, where you can offer some valuable assistance.

Over time, you probably find that some of your own habits get in the way. Perhaps you are impatient and don't give a shrub a chance to flower, pulling it out unnecessarily; perhaps you do not pay attention to detail, regularly treading on delicate plants. If you care enough, you begin to change those personal habits and find with great satisfaction that some of these changes reach into other areas of your life. You also find that other qualities are useful. You find that you have an eye for form and shape and can recognize and remember any new plant immediately.

As your grasp of gardening increases, other things begin to become obvious. You notice details—cycles and rhythms that you hadn't observed before. You begin to see patterns—clusters of plants, trees, grasses, and insects that seem to function as wholes—

as miniature ecosystems. And you begin to appreciate the impact of the larger context on the gardens where you work. You see that what you do is connected to other features of your world in myriad ways. Through your garden, you even begin to learn about other things, such as digestion, chemical functions, connectedness in ecological balance, and process and change. You explore and learn with Robin, who has now become a good friend.

And through the doing, the learning, and the creativity, you also find yourself acquiring an unexpected peace of mind. You experience something intrinsically joyful in simply being in the garden. You find that design, for instance, is not just a clever idea imposed from the outside, but involves a relationship with the garden. You possess an inner sense of a "good fit," a way of gardening that is peculiarly suited to you. The feeling is one of coming home.

Aspects of Cognitive Horizons for the Perceptual Orientations

The allegory of the gardener reveals a set of characteristics in a teacher that helped to greatly enrich the learning experience. These characteristics point to a distinction between Perceptual Orientations 1 and 3 and highlight the transition that guides Perceptual Orientation 2. We grouped the characteristics into five main areas:

- Subject matter craftsmanship
- Respect for student purposes
- An awareness of possibilities
- A sense of process
- A grasp of interconnectedness and wholeness

Subject Matter Craftsmanship

Every good teacher that we have met had genuine mastery of some domain or subject area. Thus, the degree of craftsmanship and appreciation of excellence is an indicator of an educator's cognitive horizon.

Craftsmanship begins with technical/scholastic knowledge. In "Adaptive Schools in a Quantum Universe," Garmston and Wellman (1995) write

> Content knowledge is insufficient to ensure high-quality instruction. Knowledge of the deeper structure of the discipline is required. Teachers' manuals and inservice sessions on teaching strategies typically do not explore this territory. The critical arenas for exploration here are: What do experts currently believe is the most valid content in a particular field? How do they think about this field? What is the path from novice to expert thinking and action in this field? (p. 11).

Craftsmanship goes beyond expertise about a subject or field, however, because it includes the skill that comes from sustained application and experience. Craftspeople have a felt meaning for a subject or area. They grasp the patterns. They know how the skill, subject, or discipline plays itself out in the world. They also understand the personal work that is needed in developing craftsmanship:

> High-performing individuals and groups strive for mastery and improvement. They persevere to resolve differences between present and desired states. They create, hold, calibrate, and refine standards of excellence. They seek elegance. They strive for precision in language and thought. They know they can continually perfect their work and are willing to pursue ongoing learning (Costa and Garmston, in Garmston and Wellman 1995, p. 9).

Perceptual Orientation 1 thinkers tend to have textbook knowledge and basic facts. Thus, they are at home when following the text but often become disconcerted when they have to abandon the text story line. This approach shows up quickly when a teacher begins a class by saying, "Now turn to page __."

Perceptual Orientation 2 thinkers know more, often taking great pride in their knowledge. For example, many acquire further college credits and complete graduate programs to obtain higher degrees in specific subjects. They tend to have a great deal of technical/scholastic knowledge, which includes a grasp of complex concepts.

Perceptual Orientation 3 thinkers both know their field and can apply their knowledge. The gardening teacher is an example. Robin had read about the subject; could recommend books, magazines, and helpful TV programs; and was a master gardener. Robin knew about plants; soils; weather conditions and climates; nutrients and fertilizers; relationships between plants and insects; and pruning techniques. We all know of examples in other domains:

• The teacher of social studies and economics who once worked at a high level in the futures market and can extend his subject to include simulated experience in the broader economy.

• The attorney who went back to teaching school and can refer to her knowledge and practice of law to help students simulate a court system for reviewing historical and present-day legal dilemmas.

• The scientists who want to work with kids, can create hands-on experiences for exploring scientific facts, and can relate those experiences to real-world dilemmas and phenomena.

We do not mean to infer that teachers must be master teachers before they can teach anything. All of us are thrown into the deep end at times. Nevertheless, we believe that within the makeup of every Perceptual Orientation 3 thinker is a discipline in which that person has genuine mastery and craftsmanship.

Student Purposes: Reasons for Living and Learning

The way an educator handles student purposes is an indicator of that person's cognitive horizon and thus perceptual orientation.

Perceptual Orientation 1 thinkers tend to ignore student purposes altogether. They create purposes for the student and follow their timetable and lesson plans. This approach is illustrated by the sort of comment we mentioned earlier: "Okay, now it's time for math. Open your books to page __."

Perceptual Orientation 2 thinkers try to both create and impose a purpose. They ask students to participate in well-orchestrated activities, with well-planned and thought-out questions and answers. These teachers are genuinely concerned for other, less involved students, but their concern takes the form of such phrases as, "This is important" or "You will need to know this at a later date." Even though they care about the students, they tend to disregard student-generated questions that appear to deviate from the subject at hand and fail to explore student-generated thoughts about specific subjects and topics. This tension can become a severe problem for sophisticated Perceptual Orientation 2 thinkers. They want to work with students' intrinsic motivation and real interests but do not know how to reconcile that effort with letting go of control and meeting curriculum mandates.

Perceptual Orientation 3 thinkers are more likely to search continually for what interests students and then seek to relate the curriculum to those interests. An example is a high school literature teacher in Australia who befriended some troubled adolescents in his class. After spending several weeks exploring personal issues such as family relationships and the problem of violence, he asked them if they might like to know how others had dealt with similar situations. This discussion led easily into both history and literature, to the extent that many of these students became interested in Shakespearian plays, the history of the time covered in those plays, and the time the plays were written.

Linking student purposes to what students learn is rewarding not only for students but also for teachers:

> The change here at Dry Creek allows me, as the teacher, to explore areas and ideas that go beyond the confining boundaries of a shortsighted textbook. Also, it allows the students the ability to connect their learning to their lives. They are afforded the opportunity to choose their destiny, be change-agents, and see how to use their information to learn to understand who they are. I love that! Each day is a meaningful event, not just time to be served (Teacher at Dry Creek Elementary School).

Another consequence of working with what students really feel is important is an opening up to deeper reasons for learning and living:

> Curriculum planning that takes the voices of children seriously represents a kind of openness. As we tell stories about our classroom, we feel that teachers need to remain open to children's

experience in the world and construct curricula that are deeply resonant with what each child knows, who each child is. We feel that teachers also need to understand that it is only the big, authentically engaging questions that create openings wide and deep enough to admit all adventurers who wish to enter (Clifford and Friesen 1993, p. 349).

The experience of life itself is magic. Beauty, mystery, awe, and appreciation are the elements of enchantment that humans revel in—elements beyond the ken of machines. And beyond the acquisition of knowledge that helps people survive and thrive in their world is the joy of being. As teachers more fully grasp the essence of wholeness and interconnectedness, they gain and can communicate to their students a deeper sense of being.

An Awareness of Possibilities

Cognitive horizons are defined in part by what people believe to be possible. Thus, people's capacity to function successfully is influenced by their grasp of detail and context. This capacity manifests itself in several ways. One is the scope of awareness at the moment of an action—what educators such as Art Combs (Combs, Richards, and Richards 1988) call our perceptual field and Ellen Langer calls mindfulness. The more that teachers can be aware of what is happening and how students are responding, the wider the scope for engaging intrinsic motivation and making experiences real.

A consequence of downshifting is a narrowing of a person's perceptual field. When threatened, people see fewer options because their perceptual field is smaller. When their perceptual field narrows, they tend to reduce their reality to a small view of what is actually available or possible. In Langer's terms, people revert to "premature cognitive commitments" or unexamined and programmed thinking. This smaller view tends to assume immense importance. Such individuals lose flexibility and creativity as the possibilities for reaction are reduced, in part because they see less.

Perceptual Orientation 1 teachers seem to be the equivalent of individuals who have downshifted. The focus on what has to be done and what has been prescribed is so great that they show almost no tolerance for diversity and almost no capacity to capitalize on deviation from basic categories.

Perceptual Orientation 3 thinkers are capable of tremendous possibility in the moment.

Openness to the moment is critical in any dynamic classroom or learning environment. Teachers express this sense of freedom and possibility in different ways:

> I no longer feel that good teaching means having the right answer—that's relieved me of an enormous burden (Teacher).

> Everything is a potential source for instruction if you look at it the right way (Teacher).

> Determined to foster continuity between personal and school knowledge, we work in a constant state of watchfulness. Children's authentic offerings are often made tentatively. Unlike David's, they can be subtle and easy to miss, but they are nevertheless vital components of a lived curriculum. . . . How could we have anticipated the amazement of Diana, a child in grade 1 who could not yet read, when she learned that the ancient Greeks had known the earth was spherical, but that people had subsequently lost that knowledge for thousands of years. They had lost precious knowledge about space, Diana's passion. She was offended by the carelessness of her ancestors, and endlessly intrigued by how we had gotten that knowledge back again (Clifford and Friesen 1993, pp. 344–347).

Going hand in glove with an awareness of possibility is creativity and inventiveness. Perceptual Orientation 3 thinkers tend to be more imaginative. They use materials, events, procedures, comments, and everyday tools—anything—to bring variety, novelty, surprise, and insight to life in the classroom and beyond. They bring a zest and magic to teaching and learning:

> And I am free. And I am truly free. And that is the thing I have discovered about me. I'm having a blast. Now, as much as I might get frustrated and talk xx's ear off after school for two hours, when

she's supposed to be taking the dog to the vet, as much as I may do that, I also recognize that I go home and I can't get off that computer on the weekend because I want to create. And after 27 years of teaching, I am more creative than I've ever been in my life (Teacher).

This freedom is what Senge (1990) calls personal mastery:

[Personal mastery] goes beyond competence and skills, though it is grounded in competence and skills. It goes beyond spiritual unfoldment or opening, although it requires spiritual growth. It means approaching one's life as a creative work, living life from a creative as opposed to a reactive viewpoint (p. 141).

Our experience is that the joy of learning and teaching is released as we all elicit and perceive the magic in moments of possibility. That joy is part of what we seek in our practice. (See *The Reenchantment of Learning* [Crowell, Caine, and Caine (1997)]).

Perceptual Orientation 2 thinkers are caught in the middle. Again, as they move toward Perceptual Orientation 3, they grasp the need to work with students dynamically. They can also be creative. Their challenge, and the point where they are likely to get stuck, is to seize upon spontaneous and apparently unrelated student behaviors or events outside the classroom and try to work them into what is happening at the moment.

A Sense of Process

To actualize and capitalize on possibilities, educators must have a sense of process, which is another aspect of cognitive horizons. More specifically, educators need a sense of how learning and understanding unfold over time—how mastery of any domain, and success with any project, evolve. Such understanding is exemplified in this teacher's reflection on teaching writing:

I care about the fact that they understand the process. . . . that they understand the stretching and the pulling and the not accepting and the fight you have to have with yourself to keep going and to keep making it productive and to keep changing it and to keep making it something that is worthwhile. They understand that process. . . . When those kids complain to me, or yesterday—started saying, "Mrs.__, we have stretched until we can't stretch anymore," the minute they said that I knew that I was making progress—and it's like it was an 'aha' for me. it was like, THAT'S IT! You're stretching. You bet! And it hurts. And the kids are looking at me like I'm crazy. And I thought, that's it, though. That's it! (Middle School Teacher).

Educators with broad cognitive horizons apply such principles of process as

- Everything takes time.
- Rhythms and cycles are everywhere.
- Development is rarely in a straight line.

Mastering new technology involves a learning curve. Teams take time to gel, as people get to know each other and become familiar with a situation. Both these activities illustrate the principles of process. Teachers at different perceptual orientations differ significantly in their grasp and appreciation of process.

Perceptual Orientation 1 thinkers tend to have a mechanistic sense of time. For example, a subject is taught for "x" number of weeks, and knowledge is displayed in an exam at the end. Another example is programmed learning, which asserts that each skill can be broken into modules, and modules should be mastered sequentially according to the specified program. This approach is expressed in the education system as a whole. Curriculum is broken into parts, to be learned sequentially, on an age-grade basis, and organized according to a strict calendar year.

Perceptual Orientation 2 thinkers have a richer sense of the complexity of learning. Skills unfold, but teachers still tend to be dominated by measurable timing and sequence.

Perceptual Orientation 3 thinkers tend to have a richer sense of process. They are like Robin in the allegory. Although they vary as individuals and do not share all the same characteristics, as a composite, they tend to have a sophisticated sense of the unfolding nature of learning. They see linear development and nonlinear relationships. They see cycles and rhythms as well as spontaneous and sudden changes. They grasp the richness of the field of development and so are not trapped by arbitrary time lines. The expert in the allegory did not just garden; this individual was a gardener.

In instruction, Perceptual Orientation 3 teachers tend to see process as natural and mirroring real life, where things are always changing. Therefore, teachers expect the curriculum and topics to change within the classroom. Everything is dynamic, although periods of closure and recognition of accomplishments do occur. There is always more to see, understand, and explore. Learning is a constant source of excitement and can lead to the expansion of talents, knowledge, and skills as readily as to self-understanding.

We are continually amazed at how deep and rich process is and look at this subject more closely in the next chapter.

A Grasp of Interconnectedness and Wholeness

The limits of people's cognitive horizons are set in part by their capacity to perceive relationship and connectedness. The bigger the picture teachers have of wholeness and interconnectedess, the more they can relate subjects and skills to other domains and to a student's personal interests. Here is an example:

> About two months ago, I started a new unit with the integrated group, which is basically based upon information. Information storage and transfer. I started it out by talking about codes and cycles and breaking them and trying to figure out how can you take this thing which makes no sense and figure out the sense that's in it. I had them break several codes in order to do that and then I had them go and actually do a little bit of research on the number of codes there are around us by saying, "Go and find a code that as a result of [its] being broken, somebody died, and go and find a code in fact that by its existence has changed a life" and stuff like that. We essentially got a whole bunch of them on the table and that led to . . . things like the code on CDs for example [or] bar codes on things in stores, [and] the genetic code—DNA. What that did is to open up a lot of [possibilities] for me to do the

next thing. I said, "As a result of all [the codes] we [identified,] I made a whole list of places around us where information is stored and transferred. They went all the way from records and CDs and tapes and computer disks to our sense of vision, our nose, where we smell, to communication between insects to a lot of stuff like that." I got a list of maybe 20 of these things. I said, "There are a lot of places where . . . codes are encountered. Find one you are interested in. Choose it. Go and research it. Find us some interesting things about it that you want to bring back to the class and come back and talk to the rest of us about it. . . . I also say if there's something you're really interested in that isn't on the list and fits here, come and talk to me, and we'll see how it works" (High School Teacher).

What we see here is that as people go deeper and deeper into an idea—any idea—there comes a point at which they see that everything is relationship. At that point, it becomes evident that any specific idea becomes a vehicle for exploring an infinite set of possible relationships in any number of fields. In short, adequate depth leads to breadth. Once a concept is really penetrated, it becomes a vehicle for introducing and linking the vastness of the potential curriculum. It therefore becomes an open-ended category of possibility.

Perceptual Orientation 1 thinkers are at home with fragmentation and separation. Teachers take for granted that subjects are taught separately. For example, math instruction may last 55 minutes, followed by social studies for 55 minutes. Both the partitioning of time and curriculum are assumed to be natural and normal.

Perceptual Orientation 2 thinkers appreciate some clear connections but maintain strong conceptual boundaries. For example, they may see links between math and physics, and they may accept larger bundles of connectedness, as is becoming evident in some current approaches to the teaching of science generally. But they maintain strong conceptual boundaries between some subjects, so that work in one domain (such as science) may seem unrelated to work in another domain (such as the language arts or literature).

Perceptual Orientation 3 thinkers tend to have a sense of dynamic unity. Unity and wholeness can express itself in many ways. Teachers at this orientation are open to the multiple possibilities of interconnectedness. They know or sense that every subject in the curriculum is a way of organizing human experience and is therefore interconnected at a deep level. Thus, they do not see the ideas in the curriculum as standing alone—they relate them to life experience, as occurred in our gardener story. Ideas are seen as tools for understanding and making sense of life. Subjects and skills may have a basic focus, but every subject is connected in multiple ways to other subjects and skills. This conscious grasp of interconnectedess is the core of the capacity to integrate the curriculum and work with complex experiences.

Summary of Differences in Cognitive Horizons

Indicators (see Figure 7.1 on p. 130) guided us in assessing the point where a person fell on the continuum that shows the extent of a person's cognitive horizons. As with indicators for self-efficacy, each indicator represents a point on the continuum, from Perceptual Orientation 1 to Perceptual Orientation 3. What was important was the cumulative "showing" of a person on the indicators. Our answers were gleaned through observations and interviews.

Levels upon levels of development are waiting for us. We relish those who point out, for instance, that formal operational thinking is clearly not the final stage of intellectual development (Alexander and Langer 1990). We would like to mention some of the avenues that await exploration as we all expand our cognitive horizons:

• Alternative modes of thinking, including what is called dialectical thinking in its different guises.

• Acceptance of paradox.

• Awareness of the power of symbol, myth, metaphor, and narrative.

• Joyful participation in thinking of possibilities and the celebration of human creativity.

• Examination of the new sciences, with their emphasis on interconnectedess, wholeness, self-organization, and evolution.

For us, one area of exploration is absolutely critical: the notion of inner process and self-reference. And that area is what we deal with in the next chapter.

FIGURE 7.1

INDICATORS OF COGNITIVE HORIZONS ALONG THE PERCEPTUAL ORIENTATIONS CONTINUUM

The Perceptual Orientation 1 End of the Continuum	The Perceptual Orientation 3 End of the Continuum
Uses specified texts as sole source of subject knowledge.	Demonstrates mastery and craftsmanship in some domain.
Disregards student purposes.	Appreciates the intrinsic importance of student purposes and the larger reasons for living.
Focuses on what is planned and prescribed, with little tolerance for deviation.	Lives life on the edge of possibility, with awareness of the potential in each moment.
Possesses mechanistic sense of time.	Grasps complexity and unfolding nature of process.
Accepts a fragmented view of curriculum and life experience.	Appreciates interconnectedness and wholeness.
Separates schooling from life.	Engages schooling with life.

8

Self-Reference and Process

Nonreflective teachers rely on routine behavior and are guided more by impulse, tradition, and authority than by reflection. They simplify their professional lives by uncritically accepting everyday reality in schools. They can then concentrate their efforts on finding the most effective and efficient means to achieve ends and to solve problems that have largely been defined for them by others. In contrast, reflective teachers actively, persistently, and carefully consider and reconsider beliefs and practices in light of the grounds that support them and the further consequences to which they lead.

—Posner 1992, p. 21

Educators at all three perceptual orientations engage in ongoing thought about what they do. The nature and depth of that thought, however, vary profoundly. The degree of access to what we call self-reference—an inner process of self-discovery and self-reflection—also varies. Both are indicators of people's perceptual orientation.

Perceptual Orientation 1 thinkers focus on what is to be done next. They want to know where to go, what to do, and how to do it. This type of thinking is almost identical to what most people do when they downshift. They concentrate on the steps needed to ensure immediate survival and maintain control. For some, concern with the next step is with them all the time. For others, the future is simply the immediate issue that they address when the current action is finished.

Perceptual Orientation 2 thinkers focus on larger plans, knowledge, and skill acquisition. Because they want to do a better job, they diligently attend to learning about new educational skills and strategies. Improving personal attributes is a second thrust and can range from using therapy to taking courses on time management to become more successful. It seems to us that many Perceptual Orientation 2 thinkers can be adept at both reflection on action and reflection in action; that is, they learn from feedback, and they can monitor their own perform-ance and adapt midstream.

As they examine themselves in more depth, Perceptual Orientation 2 thinkers meet an intellectual and personal challenge. That challenge is reflected in these words from one teacher:

> Life would be so much easier without self-reflection—less reward-ing, less interesting, but easier (Middle School Teacher).

Perceptual Orientation 3 thinkers may have the same concerns as Perceptual Orientation 1 and 2 thinkers, but they also focus equally on the internal process of self-reference to learn about who they are. The primary objective is a deeper awareness and sense of self. Embedded in their sense of self is their perception of the kind of person they are. Such considerations do not begin or end with a specific event, action, or occasion. Perceptual Orientation 3 thinkers have begun to notice that everything they do is the proper object of their attention and awareness, and that everything is always in process:

> The process of self-discovery that we are all involved with is not a straight one, nor are there steps that lead the way. There are ups and downs, ins and outs, frustrations and revelations. The key for my students and myself is self-reflection. We engage in thinking (not an easy step) about the "whys" and "because." In fact, I am sometimes referred to as the "why teacher" (Middle School Teacher).

> Before, I seldom stopped and pondered why, but now it is like eating and breathing; it is an integral part of my being a teacher/learner. Perhaps that statement is most important—my

students and I are all teacher/learners together (Middle School Teacher).

Our question, then, has to do with the scope of self-reference and how it is manifested in the three perceptual orientations. In particular, is anything specific required for changes in thinking to occur?

First Steps

We were clear from the beginning that our overall process was not simply a matter of people acquiring new strategies and more information. We were certain that an inner shift needed to take place; we were equally certain that it could not be forced or planned sequentially. It would have to result from some form of inner-directed process that was accompanied by action in the real world. Our objective was to set self-reference in motion in educators. How?

In the early stages, we knew that for people to willingly examine their assumptions, they needed to feel safe. Thus, we worked with their perceptual fields (see Chapter 6). When people downshift, their perceptual field is narrowed. When they feel safe and relaxed and begin to acquire self-efficacy, it is expanded. They can then become more aware of what is happening externally and internally. Providing that safety is one function served by the process groups.

A second element included a study of our brain-based learning theory. We introduced it into the process groups in the beginning because we knew that people needed to examine their own experiences with learning to grasp how the brain learns. Our theory provided the seed thoughts and frames of reference for reflection about learning.

Everyday Self-Reference

The degree of metacognitive control a teacher has over knowledge about reading instruction seemed to distinguish between teachers who can do it and those who cannot.
> —Roehler, Duffy, Conley, Herrman, Johnson, and Michelsen 1987, p. 4

Learning involves a feedback loop. People do something; get feedback about what happened or how what they did worked; make decisions based on that feedback and on their evaluation of what happened; then make further adaptations or changes. All learning, therefore, involves an opportunity for change. The ability to change depends on the extent of one's self-reference. Everyday self-reference refers to one's capacity to reflect on action, reflect in action, and engage in reflective intelligence.

Improving Skills: Reflection on Action

Donald Schon (1983, 1987) is a primary source for current notions on reflective practice. He believes that high-level professionalism in any domain is a result of different kinds of experience accompanied by reflective practice.

One part of everyday self-reference is reflection on action. For Schon, reflection on action means that after a person acts (whether an athlete or an architect), feedback is supplied, usually by an external source, and can then be used by the person to self-monitor and improve. For example, professional football players reflect on their actions when they watch videos of their performances. In education, reflection on action is what teachers do when they partner with colleagues or critical friends. These activities help them see what they are doing so that they can become aware of patterns that need to be maintained or changed. Here, for instance, is part of an interview Geoffrey Caine had with a high school teacher:

> **Teacher:** The teacher training portion—the whole pedagogy issue—I didn't really buy into it. It was only after coming here and being around people who talked about this, who really understood some of this, or who were willing to ask questions, that I began to see the validity of it and the real power of these ideas. So I think you have to have a climate whereby you can examine your practice.
>
> **Geoffrey:** Wonderful. So you do monitor and reflect on your own practice?

Teacher: Constantly.

Geoffrey: Individually and with other colleagues?

Teacher: Yes. It's amazing how much. I can't imagine teaching without that now because it has helped me grow as a learner. And I think that's a key. I see myself as much of a learner as the students. And I try to communicate that with them right away. And show that and model it. It's so foreign to what most of these kids have ever seen in their schooling, but it places me in a position where now I'm constantly questioning what's happening. And if you're doing that, I think the emergence is very natural. It occurs when it needs to occur. When I have something that is not making any sense, I get feedback from my students that this is just not working. Rather than becoming defensive, I say, "Okay. What's going on?" I'll ask colleagues about it, and it has helped me grow in ways that I could never imagine.

Improving Skills: Reflection in Action

A second part of everyday self-reference that helps improve skills is what Schon calls reflection in action—a person's capacity to observe his performance while it is going on, to assess what is happening, and to make changes midstream. Public speakers and comedians reflect in action when they gauge an audience's response and change accordingly. Athletes reflect in action when they sense their posture, movement, rhythm, and technique. All of it involves anticipating what needs to happen and assessing "on the run." A teacher's comment illustrates this idea:

> [A] teacher [is] not a fixed entity. We must constantly listen, predict, risk, observe, dictate, orchestrate, etc., as must the students. We are all in this together (Letter from a K–12 Teacher).

Schon (1987) describes how good jazz musicians reflect in action:

> When good jazz musicians improvise together, they similarly display reflection in action smoothly integrated into ongoing performance. Listening to one another, listening to themselves.

They "feel" where the music is going and adjust their playing accordingly. . . . As the musicians feel the directions in which the music is developing, they make new sense of it. They reflect in action on the music they are connectively making—though not, of course, in the medium of words (p. 30).

Metacognition and Reflective Intelligence

A third part of everyday self-reference is the ability to gain a sense of how one functions and what one's attributes and characteristics are. This type of processing engages what Gardner (1985) calls intrapersonal intelligence. A more recent source that adds significantly to this notion is what Perkins (1995) calls reflective intelligence:

[Reflective intelligence involves] coming to know your way around decision making, problem solving, learning with understanding, and other important kinds of thinking. . . . The stuff you get is very diverse—strategies, habits, beliefs, values, and more—but it's all part of knowing your way around (p. 236).

[Reflective intelligence includes] factual knowledge, mental images, values, feelings, and flexible composition of all of these into new patterns of action to suit the occasion (p. 242).

Perkins (1995) shows that most people do have a sense of how they function and of some of their propensities, strengths, and weaknesses. He uses decision making to illustrate this capacity, because most adults both know that decision making is important and have a "grab bag of tactics" for doing better:

- Give it time.
- See how your feelings change.
- Don't give way to a false sense of urgency. . . .
- Ask yourself when you really need to decide. Can you buy time?
- Figure out what your most important goals are.
- Trust your feelings.
- Get more information.
- Check your information. . . .
- Use your imagination: What would this option be like? (p. 245).

Thus, the central component of reflective intelligence is the capacity to be conscious of oneself. It is illustrated by such comments as the following extracts from anonymous teacher surveys:

I'm judgmental about people making slow progress.

I'm flexible and willing and am able to take chances, but not in front of other professionals. . . . I'm a chicken.

Perkins shows clearly that reflective intelligence is learnable. People can increase their capacities to be aware of their characteristics, and they can use this awareness to be more effective in action and capable of more complex action. Teachers in the schools where we worked showed this capacity:

I like my own personal growth—the validation of my belief system about education is forming a whole. The bits and pieces are becoming clearer. I'm challenged and excited about the journey (Middle School Teacher).

Deep Self-Reference

A deeper and more subtle type of awareness than everyday self-reference also exists. Several teachers we have quoted hint at this depth. At the deeper level, many contexts in which people live give them opportunities to change and transform themselves by paying attention to how they manage their learning, react to a task, or handle pressure. It seems to us that the deeper level must be reached to affect the personal transformation that leads to profound perceptual shifts.

One label for this deeper level of awareness is mindfulness. Let us explore it by first discussing its opposite. Ellen Langer (1989) of Harvard University demonstrated in countless experiments that often, and at a basic level, people do not think about what they are doing. She calls this lack of thought mindlessness: People act automatically and out of habit. We all experience this automaticity to some extent in the routines that we get into, say, when we are driving or in our relationships with the same people over a long period of time. When we have set beliefs and set modes of perception, we are locked into what Langer calls category traps or "premature cognitive commitments."

Mindfulness is the opposite. In the words of Thich Nhat Hanh (1976), "mindfulness" refers to "keeping one's consciousness alive to the present reality" (p. 11). More prosaic, but making the same point, Csikszentmihalyi (1990) says that a crucial element is paying attention to what is happening. For our purposes, the crucial element is that mindfulness includes being conscious of one's inner reactions in relationship to outer activity. That awareness of self in relationship is the core of self-reference.

Opening the Space of Observation

It is easy for people to be caught in a state of mind that is counterproductive and limits their enthusiasm, joy, or sense of competence. As they practice deep self-reference, the distance between perception and automatic response increases. They seem to have more space and time to observe themselves reacting. One element of mindfulness is to take the time and possess the awareness to note this inner state, catch it, and change an automatic response. A beautiful illustration comes from a student at Peninsula Middle School:

> When 10:15 came around sometimes, and math time came, I just kind of . . . whatcha call it, it's like a . . . a reaction of, "Oh no, it's math. I don't want to do math." But then . . . you know, it's just a kind of thing you do, and then I say, "Wait a minute. Ease up. There's nothing wrong with it, so go ahead and do your math" (laughs) (Fadiman 1988).

The student goes on to reflect on how he has programmed himself to think that math is hard, and that actually it can be fun. He is demonstrating a capacity to monitor his own reactions. By being aware of them, he can change them.

Perceptual Orientation 3 thinkers can access a capacity to observe themselves, their actions, and their thoughts without being tied to such observations too deeply and without identifying with them too much.

They have begun to loosen the holds that their egos and "programming" have on them. This loosening gives them immense freedom because it is part of what opens them to possibilities:

> I am capable of more change than I had thought possible (Teacher).

Another way of describing the capacity for people to observe their own reactions is "live in the question," which is what we mean by keeping an open mind. The dialogue process, which we describe in *Education on the Edge of Possibility* (Caine and Caine 1997), can help people reach openness. Let us refer to some of the guidelines for dialogue articulated by Isaacs (1993):

- Suspend assumptions and certainties.
- Observe the observer.
- Listen to your listening.
- Slow down the inquiry.
- Be aware of thought.
- Befriend polarization (p. 3).

These suggestions are variations on a theme. When people let go of their taken-for-granted ways of thinking and reacting and put them at a distance to observe, they can decide whether they wish to change or not. The process of observing oneself is both subtle and demanding. The more downshifted people are, for instance, the more committed they are to defending their basic beliefs and acting on the basis of old, deeply entrenched impulses—hence, the more reluctant they are to examine what is behind their thoughts and activities.

Our experience is that people need both time and guidance to adequately master the inner process of self-reference. In *Making Connections* (Caine and Caine 1991), we suggest that a process of contemplation developed by Gendlin (1981), what he calls focusing, is a good way to begin. The art of meditation is another. In general, as Hanh (1976) says:

> If you want to know your own mind, there is only one way: to observe and recognize everything about it (p. 37).

The objective is to free the observer (oneself) to become aware of the deep beliefs and preconceptions that govern perception and reaction. Within this open space, people can observe the deeper frames of reference that organize their perception. Such observations include the categories that they naturally use to organize experience, mental models, deep beliefs and assumptions, and hidden purposes.

Reflection is at the heart of recognizing the breach between what people say they do (espoused theories) and what their moment-to-moment actions say about them (mental models or theories-in-use). By becoming aware of their actions and recognizing how these are or are not congruent with their explanations, people begin to create the possibility for genuine change.

An example of how we introduce the tension between espoused theories and mental models is found in *Mindshifts* (Caine, Caine, and Crowell 1994). It begins with a set of general questions, such as, "What is learning" and "Where is school?" We expand on such questions by asking more detailed questions. The detailed questions use phrases that focus on the differences between espoused theories and theories-in-use (mental models). For example, the questions that follow have two possible answers. One answer reflects an espoused theory; the other, a theory-in-use:

Is school really any place where people learn [espoused theory], or any building or institution where a teacher works [theory-in-use]? We may say that students "learn" in school but our behaviors are actually guided by the belief that school is a place where I (the teacher) work. Therefore, I organize my days and weeks around "doing a job" and "working hard." Student learning is seen as deeply tied to my mental model of "students learn when I work hard." Related, of course, is "student learning is tied to student work." Genuine learning is "espoused" because it is not acted upon.

Is learning really the individual construction of meaning [espoused theory], or the coming to a conclusion that a teacher has already reached [theory-in-use]? When we explain that students are encouraged to arrive at their own conclusions and meanings, how is this congruent with the teacher's actions guided by a lesson plan and behavioral objectives that preclude student freedom to search for meaning? How can prescriptive teaching (action) facilitate genuine meaning making (what the teacher says she is doing)?

Do we really want our students to be individuals [espoused theory], or to conform to those procedures and practices that make our lives as educators more comfortable [theory-in-use] (p. 9)?

Authenticity

As people become more aware of the beliefs and assumptions that drive them, they can access their mental models. They can become aware of the dissonance between what they say and what they do. And with that awareness comes the capacity to change and align espoused theories and theories-in-use. That work is how authenticity develops. To be authentic, therefore, begins with being honest with oneself.

We knew from what we had learned about the human brain and people's capacity to learn that something was blocking the ability to access the billions of neurons waiting to be utilized. The notion of downshifting led us to believe that the gateway to more of people's potential lay in the emotions. Walking through that gateway means facing oneself. Living on the edge of possibility means that with few exceptions, this journey through one's own fears, limitations, and assumptions is essential.

Cautionary Note

The process carries with it a warning. As Perkins (1995) points out, people identify with their basic beliefs. Thus, when their beliefs are confronted, their ego-identities are challenged. That confrontation can be threatening and intensely emotional. Similarly, Combs (Combs et al. 1988) points out that it can be painful. Most of us require a moderate degree of fantasizing about reality, even if the fantasies have little to do with what others perceive. Being authentic requires a strong sense of self—a self that is both coherent, consistent, and yet capable of change given appropriate understanding.

This personal challenge is all the more reason why a process that provides safety and invites openness needs to be in place, and why people need to be able to trust those with whom they are in process. Such tension is also why shifting a person's mental model cannot be forced.

Making the transition to Perceptual Orientation 3 is also not something that happens all at once. One reason that quick fixes do not work with educational restructuring is that people need time to become aware of possibility and openness. We do as much as we can to maintain the group process—every week, every month, every year—no matter what else we do, because that process has become our vehicle for maintaining the conditions that facilitate transformation.

As mindfulness unfolds, people begin to reduce reliance on blame and the extent to which they objectify feelings and reactions. Such work means that they do not automatically blame forces or individuals in that world "out there" for what they are experiencing. To experience genuine mindfulness, people have to move beyond thinking that the "out there" is controlling or determining how they feel and behave. They begin to see how they are and can be in charge of their own thinking. In our experience, this process is how individual teachers arrive at greater self-efficacy:

> At this stage in my life, I have learned to trust myself. Western man seeks solutions externally and that seems to be a driving force in this culture. I have finally come to the realization that the answer to what I seek is within me. This has taken a lifetime of learning (High School Teacher).

Trusting in oneself does not mean that people absolve themselves of responsibility for what they do. Rather, they take charge of the way they experience the world. That type of responsibility is why self-efficacy is critical for the practice of mindfulness. The temporary suspension of ego allows the self to more or less dispassionately observe how thoughts, actions, and assumptions are being expressed and if they are congruent with what is happening "out there." This kind of evaluation leads to an awareness or wakefulness and moment-to-moment responsiveness that allows for continued deep-level change to take place.

Learning and the Experience of Flow

The learning that we describe becomes continuous. The people whom we regard as Perceptual Orientation 3 thinkers tell us that they are always learning. Learning is never ending:

> I will never "arrive" and that is fine (Middle School Teacher).

> I have so much to learn, and I'm willing to do the really hard work and painful stuff to make it happen (Middle School Teacher).

> I am always learning. I am always seeing more (Elementary School Teacher).

There is no end in sight to their learning, and they would not have it any other way. As we listen to them, we bear in mind what has almost become a platitude, namely, that we all ought to be lifelong learners. And we ask ourselves: Is this another sphere in which people might use the same words and yet mean very different things?

It seems to us that the type of learning that these teachers are describing differs fundamentally from the notion that people should always be mastering new skills or acquiring new information. In addition to talking about becoming more competent, they seem to be describing a process of reflection and growth of self that is intrinsically rewarding and fulfilling. Though painful at times, this self-referential learning is joyful. In the words of one colleague: "This [constant reflection] is the place where I live."

The experiences described correspond closely to what Csikszent-mihalyi (1990) calls flow:

> "Flow" is the way people describe their state of mind when consciousness is harmoniously ordered, and they want to pursue whatever they are doing for its own sake (p. 6).

Csikszentmihalyi points out that "playing with ideas is extremely exhilarating" (p. 127):

If "normal" scientists are motivated by their work, "revolutionary scientists"—the ones who break away from existing theoretical paradigms to form new ones—are even more driven by enjoyment (p. 135).

The sheer joy of learning seems to be a characteristic of Perceptual Orientation 3 thinkers—the joy that Csikszentmihalyi describes. He also found that every flow activity

provided a sense of discovery, a creative feeling of transporting the person into a new reality. It pushed the person to higher levels of performance, and led to previously undreamed of states of consciousness. In short, it transformed the self by making it more complex. In this growth of the self lies the key to flow activities (p. 74).

There is a punch line. Joy makes learning an end in itself. Learning does not have to be imposed, forced, or externally motivated. At the same time, joy is accompanied by the growth and increasing complexity of a person. The consequence is that the capacity to understand and perform at increasingly higher levels is natural and self-generating. The meaning of hard work is forever altered.

Ultimately, that development is what we want in children:

The rapt concentration on the child's face as she learns each new skill is a good indication of what enjoyment is about. And each instance of enjoyable learning adds to the complexity of the child's developing self (Csikszentmihalyi 1990, p. 47).

Perhaps the greatest cause for sadness in education is the loss of the joy of learning. Csikszentmihalyi suggests that it dissipates quite early in most children. It is clearly absent in vast numbers of adults working in education. Although our objective was to understand and then improve teaching and learning, we have found that clarifying the relationship between the reflective process and the sheer delight in learning wonderfully rewarding. In-depth self-reference ignites intrinsic motivation. Perhaps the single most joyful characteristic of our work with our schools and teachers has been the ongoing laughter that accompanies our working together.

Self and Others

Whenever one speaks of self-reference, there is the danger that it will be construed as an argument for self-indulgence and narcissism. That fear is well founded because of past events. For example, consider what happened in many therapy groups in the '70s. Individuals engaging in weekend "encounters," freshly armed with a new freedom to do their own thing, were all too often left without a deeper understanding of how their needs were linked to their community and responsibilities to others. Such freedom was heady indeed for the offspring of those who lived the puritan ethic of working hard, and may have contributed to the "what's-in-it-for-me" culture. The self-reference we speak of, however, is the opposite of self-indulgence. It is a constant questioning of self, rather than a constant reiteration of self-interest. Self-reference also carries a deep sense of responsibility for one's own growth and that of others. Individual growth is connected to and facilitates the whole system.

Why does self-reference not simply degenerate into self-indulgence? The answer takes us back to systems and the idea of wholeness. We contend throughout this book that everything is both separate and interconnected. Indeed, things are not just interconnected, but also a part of everything else. We refer the reader to the various references to the "web" of life in Chapter 1. A single mother struggling for survival may not concern society directly, but a society made up of children whose bodies are programmed for hunger and fear is a society where life is affected negatively.

The idea of interconnectedness is counterintuitive in our culture. Dualistic beliefs lead to the notion that body and mind, you and I, are necessarily separate. Mechanism becomes possible as a mode of thought because it carries with it the sense that each part is separate. These memes—these extraordinarily compelling ideas—act as filters that shape how people perceive everything. That perception includes what Russell (1995) calls our self-model. A person's image of how she fits in the world, and of what it means to be a person, is grounded in a set of beliefs about separateness.

When people first begin to relax their minds and examine themselves in depth, and when they open their minds to the possibility that life offers more, they become aware that because everything is a part of everything else, each one must necessarily also be a part of the whole. We are not totally separate entities—feeling compassion for others becomes natural. What we find is that as people explore their thoughts, reactions, and beliefs, they are obliged to examine their interactions with others. And the deeper they go, the more they find that they understand others. As a consequence, the notion of self begins to change. They begin to realize that they are all expressions of each other and that what they do to others in some way they do to themselves.

Joseph Jaworski, founder of the American Leadership Forum and author of *Synchronicity: The Inner Path of Leadership* (Jaworski 1996), had such an insight after a discussion with physicist David Bohm:

> Bohm's conversation with me was like a bolt of lightning. . . . We were talking about a radical, disorienting new view of reality which we couldn't ignore. We were talking about the awareness of the essential interrelatedness and interdependence of all phenomena—physiological, social, and cultural. We were talking about a systems view of life and a systems view of the universe. Nothing could be understood in isolation, everything had to be seen as a part of the unified whole (p. 80).

That grasp of interconnectedness triggers a major shift in a person's sense of responsibility and contribution. In principle, injuring another person is as pointless as having one hand attack the other.

The awareness of interconnectedness has a powerful and practical consequence for educators. The way to radically benefit children is for teachers to transform themselves as people. That transformational process can be taken as far as the individuals and the community wish.

Implications of Self-Reference

In our experience, the inward search—the process of self-reference—is crucial for a shift to Perceptual Orientation 3, and it is a process that Perceptual Orientation 3 thinkers intentionally and consistently work on. We found several practical consequences when people were able to make the shift:

• The capacity to observe oneself leads to more open-mindedness, and open-mindedness helps people tolerate ambiguity and diversity and to live with uncertainty. Open-mindedness helps people refrain from responding too quickly to a child, which supports the capacity to develop wait time. They are more comfortable with divergent questions and problems that do not have simple right or wrong answers. Because open-minded people tend to live on the edge of possibility, they are more likely to be open to multiple possibilities in any moment and experience. Open-mindedness is the open space that allows for new ideas and possibilities to emerge. And, we suggest, the degree of people's open-mindedness marks their capacity to change and learn.

• In a Perceptual Orientation 1 system, people change the system by doing things to it and to others. In a Perceptual Orientation 3 system, people become aware that by changing themselves, they actually contribute to a change in the system.

• As we explain in *Education on the Edge of Possibility* (Caine and Caine 1997), a core ingredient in self-organization of complex adaptive systems is the type of self-reference in which participants engage. The greater the capacity of each self to understand the interconnectedness of all, the more others will be treated as part of the self. Thus, self-reference naturally begins to include others.

Summary of Differences in Self-Reference

We looked for indicators (see Figure 8.1 on p. 148) to show the differences in self-reference among the perceptual orientations. As with the indicators for self-efficacy and cognitive horizons, each indicator represents a point on a continuum, from Perceptual Orientation 1 to Perceptual Orientation 3.

FIGURE 8.1
INDICATORS OF SELF-REFERENCE ALONG THE PERCEPTUAL ORIENTATIONS CONTINUUM

The Perceptual Orientation 1 End of the Continuum	The Perceptual Orientation 3 End of the Continuum
Takes pride in formal knowledge and in knowing what students need to know.	Sees self as learning constantly, with students and others as teachers.
Derives joy, which is results based, from success.	Derives joy in the moment-to moment process of teaching and learning.
Focuses on what needs to be done next.	Is open to multiple possibilities, including possibilities in the moment.
Bases learning and need to learn on outcomes or action and the need to change skills.	Includes the need for further personal transformation.
Does not self-correct readily, particularly during action.	Is sufficiently aware to monitor performance and change midstream.
Cannot readily see another's point of view or another course of action.	Is open to multiple perspectives within a coherent frame of reference.
Uses others' comments and opinions as the criteria for defining self.	Reflects on own actions and self-corrects on the basis of these.

Perceptual Orientation 1 thinkers' ability to reflect and process experience focuses on what is to be done next. They have little understanding that personal and intellectual growth is part of an orderly process. Questioning of, and participation in, re-visioning current practices or systemic processes are extremely rare. They interpret change through the lens of loyalty to an external authority and generally see change as threatening to the status quo.

Perceptual Orientation 2 thinkers' ability to reflect and process experience extends to skill development and reflection upon personal qualities and abilities. Perceptual Orientation 1 thinkers moving into

Perceptual Orientation 2 may experience discomfort as the understanding of their own growth becomes real. Fear of letting go of old patterns and mindsets and dependence on outside authority may also make them volatile. Such experiences are also reasons why most individuals decide not to go ahead with further explorations into brain-based learning.

Perceptual Orientation 3 thinkers tend to be reflecting on and processing experience on an ongoing basis, and tend to view themselves in terms of personal transformation. They also live in paradox. On the one hand, they have a strong sense of self. On the other, they see themselves in relation to others and a greater whole. They see change on multiple levels as orderly and natural. They are at home with the "Hermeneutic Spiral," consisting of experience, self-reference that informs experience, and new applications or enlarged understanding. They grasp, if only intuitively, that as they learn more they become more complex and the possibilities for their own continued evolution increase.

9

From Control to Building Relationships That Facilitate Self-Organization

Control: exercise authority over; to direct; to command; to hold back; restraining; curb.

—*World Book Dictionary* 1979

Letting go of control is so scary.

—Teacher

We frequently found that even when teachers had high self-efficacy, were broadening their cognitive horizons, wanted to engage in a more constructivist approach to learning, and were engaging in self-reflection, they had great difficulty facilitating rather than directing or controlling the learning of their students. And although none of the changes necessary for Perceptual Orientation 3 are easy, letting go of control is the one change the majority of teachers identified as most difficult.

What is it about control that is so important? To control means to regulate. Why would anyone who cares for others feel the need to regulate them? One answer is that control is for the children's own good. And, of course, there is truth in this answer. Whether or not children understand why they need to use a toilet, or why parents set boundaries and prohibit ingesting certain things, does not matter. What matters is that children do what they are told because to not do so is dangerous or outrageously unacceptable.

At the same time, we all know that children are curious and spontaneous, and that these attributes should be fostered. After all, such traits are what drives children to imitate language, try things out, and find out about their world. Hence, as parents, we seek to balance control with freedom. Our efforts of control, then, need to act like a flexible container, where children can safely explore.

Educators are constantly forced to engage in the same set of choices. A tension exists between nurturing and supporting freedom and creative exploration on the one hand, and establishing controls and inducing delay of gratification and respectful behavior on the other. The difference between Perceptual Orientation 1 thinkers and Perceptual Orientation 3 thinkers lies in what they consider to be primary. Perceptual Orientation 1 emphasizes control; Perceptual Orientation 3 emphasizes creative exploration. As already pointed out, however, a Perceptual Orientation 3 approach is not the equivalent of laissez-faire. It must also deal with order. The solution inevitably turns out to be some mode of facilitated self-organization. The Perceptual Orientation 3 approach, it seems to us, is essential for education of the future, because the Perceptual Orientation 1 approach has become self-defeating—it inhibits natural, spontaneous self-organization based on purposes and meanings.

We therefore found that the control used to make students do what is required to achieve the teacher's goals is different from orderliness that comes from small communities of learners pursuing meaningful goals and purposes.

The Problem: Seeing Classrooms and Schools as Machines Rather Than as Living Systems

All this time, we have created trouble for ourselves in organizations by confusing control with order.

—Wheatley 1992, p. 22

Traditionally, all systems were conceived of as machines, including social systems such as education. They were designed to be stable and unchanging. And the ideal state was one of equilibrium. In short, they were designed to be controllable. Perceptual Orientation 1 is grounded in this view of systems.

An emerging body of knowledge is providing educators with a much better understanding of how systems work. We explore this knowledge in some depth in Chapters 2 and 3 in *Education on the Edge of Possibility* (Caine and Caine 1997) and deal with some core issues here.

We now know that most systems are more dynamical. Several terms are used to describe them. Self-organizing systems, living systems, and complex adaptive systems are examples. We use the label complex adaptive systems. They are full of energy; they interact with the environment; they are open. Indeed, their existence and resilience depend on having energy and room for change. In the jargon of the new science, the ideal state for system adaptation is the edge of chaos—what we call the edge of possibility. An exchange of information and energy with the environment is constant:

> For a system to remain alive, for the universe to move onward, information must be continually generated. If there is nothing new, or if the information that exists merely confirms what is, the result will be death. Isolated systems wind down and decay, victims of the laws of entropy. The fuel of life is new information—novelty— ordered into new structures. We need to have information coursing through our systems, disturbing the peace, imbuing everything it touches with new life. We need, therefore, to develop new approaches to information—not management but encouragement,

not control but genesis. How do we create more of this wonderful life source? (Wheatley 1992, pp. 104–105).

Command and control work well (although people pay a price) when systems are so stable that they function like machines. They become self-defeating in volatile conditions and as a system moves toward the edge of possibility. Let us explore this tension.

Purpose of Control: To Guarantee Learning Outcomes

Public education is a venture that taxpayers fund and communities administer. In a product outcome society, these "investors" feel that they have a right to a set of learning outcomes, and indeed they do. Basic skills and knowledge are critical. This kind of thinking leads to expectations that can be spelled out and measured with certainty and predictability. Such thinking is compatible with the movement toward accountability of educators and with the implementation of national standards based solely on standardized test scores.

The primary reason for the effort spent on control is that educators are trying to guarantee learning outcomes. From one perspective, specifying outcomes in detail and applying them at different levels— from national standards to curriculum frameworks to lesson plans— make sense. For example, if teachers want students to develop a keen sense of history, then spelling that outcome out is reasonable. We have done the same thing by identifying what we believe are the essential attributes for functioning in a fluid and emergent system.

What Is Being Controlled?

Perceptual Orientation 1 thinking seeks to control at least three arenas in a classroom:

• ***Curriculum: what is taught.*** Traditionally, teachers regard curriculum as what is to be learned. We discuss this topic in Chapter 2 of *Education on the Edge of Possibility* (Caine and Caine 1997) when we point out that "the curriculum is separated by subject; and there tends to be a set of core subjects," with others as secondary or elective

(p. 45). Each subject is assumed to have a logical developmental sequence, with one segment treated in each year of a student's education. The *California Social Science Framework* (California State Board of Education 1988) makes this sequence explicit. Thus, grade 7 deals with the medieval and early modern world to 1769; grade 8 deals with U.S. growth and conflict, 1783–1914; grade 10 focuses on the modern world 1789 to present; and so on. We see all of this selection, partitioning, and organizing as acts of control at the Instructional Approach 1 level.

• ***Instruction: how to teach.*** Instruction refers to the way that students are led to interact with the content prescribed by the mandated curriculum. An enormous amount of the effort invested in educational maintenance and reform is directed to this end. This effort includes inservice training; mastery of new instructional strategies; concern with pedagogy and instruction; and the lesson plans that contain organized material, devised activities, practice and rehearsal techniques, and testing.

• ***Behavior that aids teaching and reduces interference.*** In the traditionalist view, what is most important is that students behave so that the acquisition of skills and facts is possible. When agencies and individuals unknown to teachers specify narrow outcomes, when quantifiable evidence of accrued learning is set, and when 30 or more students per class are geared to expect an authoritarian environment, then teachers have to keep tight control over what is being done to and by students. Teachers therefore take charge of such decisions as where tables and desks are placed and how students should interact with one another. Talking, movement, and on-task behavior are defined. This entire enterprise is supplemented by the discipline policy. The classroom control is embedded within a larger context of logistical parameters that educators and the community control. These decisions include the design of school buildings, allocation of classrooms, number of students in each class, grade levels, class periods, and teacher and staff responsibilities. All in all, an enormous amount of effort and energy is spent controlling what happens in schools and classes.

The problem, as we see it, is that the most important outcomes cannot be programmed or produced. They have to emerge. Even a "keen sense of history" cannot be taught as information or a skill. It has to evolve out of student experience that is facilitated and processed appropriately over a significant period of time. Our view is that world-class standards in any complex sphere, whether science, math, literature, or music, emerge when student passion is ignited, nurtured, and guided.

For that emergence to occur, a particular dynamic needs to exist, and the problem of Perceptual Orientation 1 thinking is that the control that it seeks places a lid on the necessary dynamic. The limitations become clearer when we look beyond the goals themselves to see what else is actually being controlled.

What Else Is Being Controlled?

As a consequence of control over curriculum, instruction, and behavior, the flow of another type of information is also being controlled. The kind of information that we are talking about is not limited to facts, knowledge, and skills, although these are included. We are referring to the dynamical information that emerges immediately—in what is called real time—from interactions between all the individuals, sources, and relationships that are engaged in a lived context. This kind of information is what teachers need to deal with directly and honestly, and it provides opportunities to invoke student learning.

What does this information look like? It shows itself in many ways:

• It is the sudden burst of enthusiasm as a group of children see a spiral rotate on a small engine and shout, "It's just like Roger Rabbit"—providing the teacher with the opportunity to ask, "Why? What are the similarities and differences you see?"

• It is the response of small children building a cardboard bathyscope and saying, "We'll take all the kids down into the ocean, but we can't take you, Mrs. ___. It might not come back up"—which can spark a question by the teacher about pressure and weight and how they could determine just who or how many could go down and come back up.

- It's in the free and open challenges students present to each other while building a museum.
- It refers to information on the Internet used to build or explore ideas.
- It's the question that a child asks an elderly school guest as he walks through the classroom: "Did you wear armor when you were young?"—allowing the guest to respond in a way that makes time and history more real.
- It's the fierce debate on the school ground about whether the Cleveland Browns football team has a right to leave Cleveland—which a skillful teacher can turn into an exploration in civics, economics, and values.
- It is the sullen boredom about the names of the U.S. presidents that is embedded in the soft remark, "Who cares?" (made in an aside to a friend by someone who did not know when George Washington was born)—leaving the teacher a chance to see disengagement as an opportunity to partner this student with one who loves history.
- It is in students' eager and all-embracing pursuit of facts about dinosaurs or cold fusion, as they bring in knowledge gleaned from the Learning Channel or newspaper articles.

Information of this kind includes the totality of lived, authentic, spontaneous response to actual experience—all the things that exemplify a sophisticated, real-life complex learning environment. Each such situation offers an opportunity for embedding and expanding new ideas and relevant facts. In most schools, however, these opportunities remain unknown, ignored, or suppressed. Thus, many student responses to what goes on in the classroom, school, and world are simply dismissed. They are treated as noise to be reduced or eliminated.

The Price Educators Pay for Excessive Control

Perceptual Orientation 1 thinking comes at a high price:

- By specifying narrow outcomes and standards that have no meaning to learners, educators reduce the chances of achieving the kinds of outcomes that they set out to generate, including those described in this chapter. They defeat themselves by creating conditions that are not conducive to meaning making. Meaning making requires dynamic and interactive conditions, and when they are suppressed, the lack of meaning reduces opportunities for students to achieve the goals and meet the high standards—the high challenges—that are critical.

• By specifying objectives so narrowly, educators blind themselves to additional skills, capacities, and purposes that are becoming indispensable in the Information Age. Students need to be equally adept at demonstrating an understanding of broad concepts; challenging ideas by questioning opinion or bias; experimenting with new ideas; taking risks in thinking; using clues in search of evidence; and thinking scientifically and rationally as well as creatively and metaphorically. They need to be able to deal with ambiguity and to question what does not make sense to them. They need to be able to identify their weaknesses and strengths and work toward goals that will help them improve. The educational process needed to attain these additional purposes is not possible in a tightly controlled environment.

• Teachers may actually generate and trigger discipline problems when they neutralize student enthusiasm and engage students in a power struggle that has little to do with learning. Such struggles are the opposite of creating conditions that naturally generate orderliness.

The Perceptual Orientation 3 Alternative to Control

Educators need an alternative to control. To clarify what it is, let us look at the possible solutions, sometimes intuitive and sometimes well thought out, that Perceptual Orientation 3 thinking offers. Perceptual Orientation 3 thinkers have a sense of how complex adaptive systems function. They enjoy and encourage movement toward the edge of possibility. They understand the organizing power of ideas, purposes, and meanings. And they facilitate the simultaneous interplay of all these elements so that they end up with self-organization:

> [Self-organization is] the ability of living systems to organize into patterns and structures without any externally imposed plan or direction. Systems self-organize without strategic plans, without leaders being visionary for others, without having to think it through ahead of time. A self-organized system emerges (Wheatley 1995, p. 4).

Many factors contribute to self-organization; one is critical for our purposes. As we know from the theory of brain-based learning, people have their own deep meanings, purposes, values, compelling beliefs, and mental models that define their perceived relationships with each other and the world. In the course of life, each person and group of people interpret what is happening to them and adjust their responses because of what they perceive is happening, given their values and assumptions (deep meaning). When any system is sufficiently dynamical and energized, then all these individual and interrelated responses and adjustments naturally result in complex and changing patterns of a fluid type of order. That is self-organization.

Perceptual Orientation 3 thinkers build relationships that facilitate self-organization, which, therefore, is an alternative to control. They recognize, often intuitively, that everything is in relationship to everything else. Thus, they also see that behavior and learning are always interconnected because people are always in relationship to each other and their contexts. They see procedures and strategies as context and purpose dependent. And all these relationships are dynamical.

What Perceptual Orientation 3 Thinkers Do

Perceptual Orientation 3 thinking makes Instructional Approach 3 possible. This capacity is manifested in the ways that self-organization is facilitated in the classroom and the school.

Build Interpersonal Relationships and Prestige

Orderliness and coherence depend on relationships between people. Indeed, one of the critical elements of a complex adaptive system is the network, web, or relationships that exist (Capra 1988, Wheatley 1992). Perceptual Orientation 3 thinkers more often than not work to increase the number and complexity of relationships between people (including students and the outside world) and between people and contexts. For them, enriching relationships is one of the hidden consequences of complex projects and cooperative learning.

At the same time, Perceptual Orientation 3 thinkers strive to strengthen their own authentic relationships with their students:

> I have less [need for creating order] here than I would have had, say, in a public school where I was before. But I think essentially the principles are the same. You'll find when you look at this that I talk about winning kids' hearts. I'm a believer that the first couple of weeks when you go into a classroom you work very hard to win kids' hearts, to get them to believe in you, that you know what you're doing, that you care about them, and that if they take your hand and trust you and walk the journey together that you're going to have a great time. And I tell my kids that I can be one of the best teachers they have if they will allow me to be (High School Teacher).

A straight lecture is more powerful if the lecturer can develop a relationship with the audience. We should add that this rapport needs to be accompanied by the lecturer's expert knowledge, which should be relevant to students and student purposes. According to Lozanov (1978a, 1978b), a combination of caring and subject matter expertise is the heart of prestige. A person with prestige commands respect and is heard differently from someone who has little expertise and is simply a figure to be obeyed or disobeyed. In his view, prestige of the instructor is indispensable to release what he calls students' "nonspecific reserves" and what we might call their potential. Prestige, then, depends on the relationship between people that emerges from an environment of congruence, empathy, and positive regard (Rogers 1969), but such an environment is initially related to the respect the student gleans from the knowledge given or provided.

Open Up Curriculum and Inquiry

> *My whole curriculum is organized around open-ended kinds of things. Very seldom is there a right answer to anything. For example, we start the year with looking at the world in 1500, and there's a*

map which the students could create where they put all kinds of stuff on it from all kinds of different sources. A student says, "This map doesn't agree with that map."

And I say, "Well, what do you think?" Then we start talking about ambiguity and sources, etc., and that there really isn't a right answer—there are a series of good ones and some not so good ones. So I really try to make everything focused around sort of key concepts like power, how it's expressed in society, continuity and change, and dialectic.

—High School Teacher

In *Education on the Edge of Possibility* (Caine and Caine 1997), we point out that a complex adaptive system thrives on the edge of possibility. In general, Perceptual Orientation 3 thinkers are constantly moving the class toward, and sustaining, this edge. They do this work with active processing and in multiple ways. Here are two examples:

• They tend to go beyond closure. When a student solves a problem, the teacher is ready with questions such as, "How could you do it differently?" or "What would happen if you changed these facts?" The Socratic method works best this way and is a powerful tool, for instance, in legal education. One main purpose of intensive active processing is that it keeps the inquiry going.

• They invite student explorations and interests. If a student shows an interest in math, for instance, a Perceptual Orientation 3 teacher can find ways to relate history and writing to build on that interest. This teacher understands that high challenge is a key to constant student inquiry.

Encourage Multiple Inputs of Information

As noted earlier in this chapter, "the fuel of life is new information. . . . We need to have information coursing though our systems" (Wheatley 1995, p. 104). Perceptual Orientation 3 thinkers understand and encourage this flow. They know how to tap into "this wonderful life source":

• They constantly introduce new information and ideas that may be relevant, going far beyond texts and curriculum specifications. For example, they may refer to interesting TV programs; bring in books and artifacts; call upon experts from the real world; and draw upon technology and telecommunications, as well as literary, scientific, artistic, and other resources to increase the flow of information. (This is one of the processes that Wheatley and others are using to assist businesses to restructure.)

• They invite input from students:

> Our curriculum work demands mindful, deliberate improvisation at such moments. . . . We mean, rather, that each child's voice can be heard, and that their speaking can make a difference to our curriculum decision making. Improvising on children's responses to our standing invitation demands a commitment to recognizing human relationship as a fundamental source of knowledge. At the beginning of the year, we could not plan for these moments, but we were prepared for them because we knew that they would inevitably arise. We knew that the children would give us what we needed to know, as long as we remained open to the possibilities (Clifford and Friesen 1993, p. 344).

Whether the interest comes from a single student or a class, these teachers invite input, even when it goes beyond what the teacher is interested in or knows. An example we use in *Making Connections* (Caine and Caine 1994a) is the story of Leo Woods, a high school chemistry teacher. After he introduced the cold fusion story to his class when it became headline news several years ago, he found students reading voraciously and bringing clippings into his 11th grade chemistry class almost daily:

• They set up projects and situations that naturally generate information exchange with the environment. For example, a teacher at the Illinois Mathematics and Science Academy set up a stock exchange program and connected all his students to the Internet. This project parallels the complex ecoliteracy projects that Capra (March 1995) sets up with schools.

• They understand that students generate information when they participate for any length of time in genuine interactions. Student

discussions, opinions, disagreements, humor, experiences, and suggestions are all sources of the information that sustains self-organization.

Integrate Learning and Behavior

Perceptual Orientation 1 thinkers believe that they must control
behavior for learning to happen. Perceptual Orientation 3 thinking is
the reverse. It is based on the belief that learning itself is an orderly
process. Hence, when meaningful learning is taking place, orderliness
naturally results:

> You know, I don't worry about a loss of control because I'm not
> sure I even have control per se. I tend to think of myself as
> facilitating rather than controlling. In terms of classroom behavior
> and in terms of staying on task, it's not a problem that we have a
> lot up here because kids love to do it [projects and tasks tied to
> meaning and purpose] almost as much as the teachers do (High
> School Teacher).

Another example comes from Michael Apple, who relates his
experience teaching filmmaking (another form of narrative) to adoles-
cent girls in a state-run corrections institution:

> Soon, everyone, everyone, was deeply involved. Magic markers
> were shared. Comments and criticism that were meant to help,
> not to cut down someone, were given by the kids to each other.
> Jokes and laughter, sighs and grimaces, calls for assistance, words
> of satisfaction and frustration also filled the air. It was at times
> noisy, at times remarkably quiet. It was the controlled chaos that
> organizes and reorganizes itself when kids are deeply involved in
> doing something that is playful and yet utterly serious to them
> (Apple, in Casey 1995, p. 237).

When students make the connection between behavior and learning, we find that they will spontaneously work beyond school hours.
They will go home and roust family members from in front of the TV
to help them build something or figure something out. They will also
visit the library, conduct computer and card catalog searches, and at
times work through lunch. School and life are not separate.

In addition, when the teacher leaves the room, unless students are engaged in an activity in which the teacher has an integral part, they will not notice that the teacher is gone. The following is an illustration that we observed:

> Students in Kelly's class are working on geometry. They are in groups and have decided to build a community, requiring certain knowledge and application of geometric design and measurement. Everyone is participating, and the feeling is intense in most groups. Some diagram, others measure, some design, and some calculate. There is a great deal of talking, of exchanging ideas. At this point, Kelly needs to leave her class to get educative feedback from classroom observers (us). To make sure that students are not left unsupervised, her principal has called in a substitute that the district hired. The substitute comes in, walking very much like a troubadour, and he is playing a mandolin. A few students notice the mandolin player, but most pursue their work. One or two students ask a question about his instrument, some ask what he does for a living (he plays in a restaurant), but almost the entire class adjusts to doing their work with lovely music.

We are not suggesting that teachers bring mandolin players into every class. We are saying that the most important criterion in Perceptual Orientation 3 is student learning. If their brains are asking questions relevant to the task, hypothesizing about outcomes, generating theories, collecting data, disagreeing about facts, searching out genuine answers, and recording them for public scrutiny, then learning is taking place at a high-challenge level. As a rule, we prefer that the teacher be present to help that level of processing take place. But if a teacher cannot be present, and students do much of the processing on their own, then we are looking at a Perceptual Orientation 3 classroom where the teacher is the top professional leader or master among mature participants and fellow learners. The leader's leaving does not interfere with self-motivated, empowered learners engaged in purposeful activity.

When enough meaning making is going on, and when the meaning is tied to student purposes, then the problems of discipline tend to fall by the wayside. The learning is what leads to order. Hence, little control is needed to make the learning happen.

Use Broader Cognitive Horizons

Because Perceptual Orientation 3 thinkers tend to have broader horizons than do Perceptual Orientation 1 thinkers, they also tend to see multiple connections between student purposes, curriculum, specific projects, and experiences. This breadth of vision provides them with a larger arena within which to operate (see Chapter 6).

Orderliness and Coherence

As already pointed out, Instructional Approach 3 is not an invitation to unorganized activity. What happens is that the broader systemic environment creates a deep sense of orderliness that is not built primarily on rules and punishment. Perceptual Orientation 3 thinkers set out to create meaningful learning and experiences that are accompanied by rhythms and routines to help sustain orderliness. Such activity can happen in classrooms, at the schoolwide level, and with the larger community:

• Projects and activities have beginnings and endings. Clarifying purposes, regrouping what has been learned, and automatically cleaning up the classroom or environment are examples.

• Jobs and responsibilities may be allocated, often on a rotating basis. The result is that individual students become responsible for seeing that many issues are attended to, including collecting materials, organizing activities and projects, and keeping records.

• The environment may be orchestrated to generate a sense of rhythm and order. Teachers may use music and art, seating arrangements that facilitate small- and large-group interactions, and lighting and temperature.

• Teachers may use some routines—behaviors and events that are both automatic and understood. Examples include developing skills for communication and conflict resolution. What matters is that the structures and routines are used to aid, not inhibit, process.

Planning

How is it possible for a teacher to be able to say the following (quoted in Chapter 3)?

> Sometimes I get nervous because I don't have a prepared lesson as I go into class. I mean, I literally don't know what to say next. But then the students ask me a question or show me what they're doing, and we're off and running. I do have a focus, even a pretty worked out long-term plan but there is no minute-to-minute predictability. The students and I create that—the moment—together (Middle School Teacher).

What the quote does not explain is the enormous amount of work that goes in to Instructional Approach 3 planning. That preparation is the context that enables "flow" in the classroom, and between the classroom and everyday life. We noticed this connection when our teachers told us that their planning and thinking about school was happening all the time. It remains the single clearest signal that a teacher is moving into Perceptual Orientation 3 thinking.

Perceptual Orientation 3 thinkers need to be able to respond to what is happening to a group of dynamic individuals at any point of the day, even though those students may have begun with some preliminary teacher or teacher/student plan. Hence, Perceptual Orientation 3 teachers have at least two levels of planning. As Ivan Barzakov expressed it (personal communication), teachers begin with a prescribed agenda, with the initial projects and activities spelled out. They also use a "floating agenda": The teacher responds to what is actually happening.

What Happens to Control in a Perceptual Orientation 3 Environment?

Because we see teaching at Perceptual Orientation 3 as an organic process where learners gather around experiences and glean and consolidate specific and collective knowledge, the teachers have to let go of controlling a specific lesson and let student interests guide learning. Teachers challenge students as the students pursue their research and demonstrate what they are learning. Once students embark on a project, Perceptual Orientation 3 teachers question, prod, and encourage dialectic thinking. Helping students master complex concepts and the formal vocabulary of a discipline becomes a primary focus. Teachers also provide information, explanations, and experiences that aid the acquisition of skills and procedures necessary for mastery. Any number of teaching strategies may be used, from ancient books to computers. The objective is to further students' understanding and enthusiasm, not provide some artificial goal or lesson the teacher has chosen independent of student purposes or meaning. We often observe learning in these classrooms to be much more like a playful and joyful exploration at the same time that learning is more intense and demanding.

Problems for Individuals Becoming Perceptual Orientation 3 Thinkers

Not all is rosy for fledgling Perceptual Orientation 3 thinkers. First and foremost, success cannot be guaranteed. Sometimes classes and groups do not self-organize in ways that are conducive to good learning, particularly if a sense of community has not been well established. We have had this experience. Second, in the early stages of enthrallment with self-organization, it is possible to become too indefinite and lax, so that not enough attention is paid to adequately setting the stage or to the practice and rehearsal that is often necessary. Keep in mind that we are talking about a way of thinking. It is quite appropriate to embed prescriptive strategies—for example, Instructional Approaches 1 and 2—in the experience of students at appropriate times.

Perceptual Orientation 2 Thinkers: Individuals in Transition

Many procedures and strategies that are introduced into education have a quality of openness that allows for some movement toward greater information flow and self-organization. Cooperative learning, for example, can become a process in which students engage in lively and challenging discussions, debates, and team work. Even when planned by teachers, complex projects and experiences permit a similar extension of input and student response. Block scheduling, peer coaching, multi-age classrooms, authentic assessment, various modes of integrating the curriculum, and the use of technology all permit a teacher to relinquish some control.

A similar note is struck with many authored or packaged materials. One by-product of moving to learning packets such as Math Renaissance and the FOSS materials (Lawrence Hall of Science 1992) is that they are inevitably accompanied by training for teachers. In the teachers we observed, such training included dialoguing about learning and teaching. As a result, these teachers tended to risk talking through their beliefs and fears and discussing how this type of teaching was different. Their discussions were similar to the way teachers interacted in our process groups. And, just as in the *Mindshifts* (Caine, Caine, and Crowell [1994]) process groups, teachers began to see the value of discussing their new impressions with each other and to value spontaneous interactions sparked by the experiences they were sharing. They also began to feel empowered as their own thoughts and ideas were valued. Thus, the freedom to question procedures and add suggestions to the teaching strategies created a new breakthrough to traditional models focused on delivery of information. Their explorations were still within a structured format, but the traditional dependence on strict adherence to a plan and outcomes had been challenged.

This change needs to be placed in perspective because it is profound, given the Perceptual Orientation 1 context of schools and the professional and intellectual isolation most teachers experience. Perceptual Orientation 2 teachers learn that the activities included in their teaching packets require a different approach. To help them feel more secure with the new format, they have their personal experiences from group discussion.

When students are engaged in cooperative experiences, time needs to be more flexible. As students consult with each other, discuss, document, and write up reports, they test and talk out varying objections and perceptions. This work often requires that parts of the experience have to be repeated, thus taking more time than is usually allowed. Placing artificial time constraints on such learning becomes unrealistic and counterproductive. As teachers realize this situation, their concept of control is often modified, and they begin to search for greater blocks of time.

The need to control learning is still high in Perceptual Orientation 2 thinkers, but they genuinely explore more complex or open-ended forms of instruction. Perceptual Orientation 2 teachers begin to believe that students can be trusted to be responsible participants in learning, provided that they are supervised to stay on task. These teachers also appear to trust themselves to participate and feel comfortable with an environment that includes more spontaneous classroom interactions, even though they still choose the curriculum and assign most time parameters. They begin to feel comfortable in situations where freedom to challenge and think freely is explored if such situations are guided by structured experiences with specified parameters. Their focus on concepts rather than topics facilitates this effort.

Summary of Differences in Self-Organization

Figure 9.1 (see p. 169) shows indicators that we used to guide us in assessing the point where a person fell on a continuum between control and the building of relationships that facilitate self-organization. Again, we caution against thinking that movement across the continuum can be imposed—it is a natural result of the process of learning, reflecting, and experimenting.

Figure 9.1
INDICATORS OF SELF-ORGANIZATION ALONG THE PERCEPTUAL ORIENTATIONS CONTINUUM

The Perceptual Orientation 1 End of the Continuum	The Perceptual Orientation 3 End of the Continuum
The extent to which individuals remarked on the importance of discipline and on the need to tell students what to do (posted rules and enforcements).	The extent to which the environment reflected a coherent community with student and teacher responsibilities and "buy in." Presence of democratic processes for decision making.
The extent to which individuals specified content, allocated times, directed student interactions, and included or excluded student suggestions.	The inclusion of student ideas to influence group or individual learning focus. How these ideas were processed both by the teacher and other students.
The extent to which individuals selected and limited feedback, assumed sole responsibility for evaluation and grading, and gave symbol grades (e.g., *A, B, C*), based on limited responses to their own questions or objectives.	The extent to which individuals encouraged student self-assessment, used authentic assessment, and extended the range of capacities and abilities that were assessed in any context.
The extent to which individuals implemented their lesson plans irrespective of student or class needs and responses.	The extent to which individuals responded to students by linking curriculum and instruction to student ideas, suggestions, needs, and interests.

10

The Perceptual Orientations and Instructional Approaches in Action

Our research shows that the instructional approaches and the perceptual orientations interact. Basically, a particular perceptual orientation makes an instructional approach possible. For example, a person with an atomistic or fragmented view of reality—what we call a narrow cognitive horizon—is not capable of deeply integrating the curriculum. Educators need broad cognitive horizons and strong self-efficacy to teach in a fluid, interconnected way that engages student purposes. Such an approach may deviate from the specific sequences that a textbook might mandate or from too literal an interpretation of state and district mandates. These interconnections are shown in Figure 5.2.

The Perceptual Orientations

We emphasize once more that the perceptual orientations are like fields. They can only be identified by grouping a number of characteristics that persist over time. Individual behavior or thinking coalesces around tendencies that can be observed and documented, as explained in Chapters 6 through 9. Although some individual differences elude any clear labeling by observers, patterns can be seen, described, and illustrated, and specific behaviors can be identified and used as indicators. We have described our approach to identifying critical characteristics of Perceptual Orientation 3 thinkers. We should add that we are NOT talking about learning styles. It is incorrect to identify a person whose style is adventurous and free flowing as being at Perceptual Orientation 3, whereas one who is more orderly and sequential is at Perceptual Orientation 2. We regard the perceptual orientations as having more in common with Piagetian stages, though the emergence of the perceptual orientations does not appear to be a linear process.

The Instructional Approaches

Similarly, sets of indicators help reveal the different instructional approaches. These indicators were spelled out in Chapter 4. The more fluid the descriptors are, the more difficult it is to work out what is going on. Establishing that teaching at Instructional Approach 3 is occurring involves direct observation of not only the teacher but also the dynamics of the entire classroom. The situation becomes even more complex because what we see as observers is colored by our own perceptual orientation.

Those not familiar with Perceptual Orientation 3 thinking are not likely to see what is really going on from a Perceptual Orientation 3 perspective. Individuals who begin by searching for specific (particularly isolated) procedures or required interactions will impose a perceptual filter when observing a self-organizing classroom, which will result in judging what is happening as being too chaotic.

We do have ways to see if teachers in fact are using a genuine Instructional Approach 3. Most important is an indication that the emphasis has moved away from the teacher and on to the students. Students should be able to answer tough questions that illustrate the sophistication of what is taking place, with most questions emerging from effective active processing. Among the more specific factors to consider are the following:

- Can students explain what they are learning when asked spontaneously?
    - Do students know why they are examining a particular topic?
    - Do students have a specific plan in mind?
    - What do students expect to find?
    - Do students have physical products or results that they can share?
    - Is there attention to details as well as to specific skills?
    - Can students explain the more specific aspects of their project?
    - Are students taking timing and deadlines into consideration?
    - Can students shift their thinking on the basis of new input?
    - Is their work for public display or performance?
    - Do students participate in the management of the class?
    - Are students courteous with one another even though lively debates and disagreements are going on?

Any learning environment where the above student capacities are evident is a classroom that inevitably has a Perceptual Orientation 3 thinker at the helm, because the type of person needed for this degree of freedom yet rigor is someone with the characteristics we described in Chapters 6 through 9.

We caution readers not to use the instructional approach seen at any point in time as the basis for assessing what type of teacher they are observing. A brain-based teacher, for example, can and does employ all the instructional approaches. Crucial differences occur, however, in how the approaches are used and integrated. For example, a major distinction exists between someone who only uses a stand-and-deliver method and one who occasionally lectures or works with memorization and specifics of skills in the context of a much larger process.

Reasons for Adopting Different Instructional Approaches

We wish to reiterate that education has both room and need for all three instructional approaches. Perceptual Orientation 3 thinking is especially important because it expands the repertoire of approaches available. Thus, people's perceptual orientation affects their grasp of learning theory and their choices about practice. Their perceptual reality governs their reading of students and the context.

A perceptual orientation can serve as a backdrop for a powerful approach to Instructional Approach 1. For example, we have met and dialogued with many people who have high self-efficacy and prefer living and working in a fluid and open-ended world; yet they have argued passionately for employing Instructional Approach 1 with certain types of students, particularly those with low self-efficacy who have grown up with a great deal of threat, creating a general sense of helplessness. The argument is that students need structure, order, and safety, and often, Instructional Approach 1 can supply these if implemented appropriately.

An illustration is afforded by Jaime Escalante, the teacher immortalized in the film *Stand and Deliver*. We would argue that he is largely portrayed as a Perceptual Orientation 2/3 thinker using Instructional Approach 1. Escalante teaches calculus, and he only occasionally integrates it into other parts of the curriculum. He does it enough however to expose his own, larger cognitive horizons, a Perceptual Orientation 3 characteristic. The school has the usual 55-minute classes, which control the amount of content to be covered. His Perceptual Orientation 3 thinking is apparent when he expands this time period by inviting students to participate in instruction before and after school. Helping students see connections between their own learning and how mathematics can be applied in their lives demonstrates further his broad cognitive horizons. Escalante is also creative in how he presents the information and rehearsal. He also uses an enormous amount of drill, and success is indicated by results on a standardized test, activities that indicate a classic Instructional Approach 1.

The larger context, however, is much richer. Escalante cares for the students and demonstrates this caring both in and out of the classroom. In such schools and classrooms, respect for the teacher's authority often borders on admiration, creating a deeper connectedness and community. The children believe that they matter. Tight parameters for what is to be learned and time limits for such learning provide security. Because such teaching permits clear and identifiable experiences of success through memorizing material—leading to clear, specifiable results—gaining self-confidence can become the road to self-efficacy. Since self-efficacy is critical for student learning, the teaching produces genuine benefits.

Examples of the Perceptual Orientations and Instructional Approaches in Operation

Much of the confusion and unrest in education stems from a clash of perceptual realities, from miscommunication between those with different perceptual orientations. We have observed just how differently the three elements of our instructional theory have been implemented. For example, one element, immersion in complex experience, can be interpreted by a Perceptual Orientation 1 thinker to mean a highly controlled activity; yet for a Perceptual Orientation 3 thinker, the same phrase suggests a sophisticated, real-life experience. Teachers may also implement the other two elements, relaxed alertness and active processing of experience, differently. The latter ranges from teacher-initiated questions with preestablished answers in a traditional classroom (i.e., Instructional Approach 1) to sophisticated, provocative invitations to justify, explain, comment, expand, debate, or clarify ongoing, student-initiated work in a brain-based environment (i.e., Instructional Approach 3).

We would like to briefly illustrate how the differences play themselves out in three arenas—technology, Gardner's (1985) theory of multiple intelligences, and whole language.

Technology

Technology is everywhere, yet what teachers actually do with it in the classroom varies enormously. As Sandy Banks and Lucille Renwick (1997) write in the *L.A. Times:*

> "Most colleges of education spend very little time and effort getting teachers good at thinking about how technology is used in the classroom," said Dave McArthur, senior computer scientist at Rand and a specialist in computers in education.

It is a waste of time and money, he said, "to have teachers do the same thing they've always done but on computer."

Still, that is precisely what is happening in many Los Angeles classrooms, even at some schools with model technology programs" (p. A29).

At Instructional Approach 1

With this approach, teachers use information technology as a simple extension of standard delivery practices. Content is fragmented, and teachers or schools maintain control.

Teachers primarily use computers to deliver information and teach basic skills through practice and rehearsal. Examples range from teaching basic operations in math and parts of the body in biology to presenting historical facts and the periodic table in chemistry. Learning involves the storing of surface knowledge.

Computer instruction tends to occur in computer labs, where groups of learners work at computers (which are frequently obsolete), in the same time block, and with identical software. Creativity and variety tend to be in the form of self-paced instruction, where students have some choice over when they use computers and how difficult they make their work. Various recording mechanisms are usually included so that teachers can monitor the number of tries, degree of difficulty, and success rates. In many schools, an independent instructor runs the computer lab, so that connection to the content of other courses is limited.

Computers may also be used for other purposes, such as word processing for completing assignments and desktop publishing for creating teacher-directed newsletters. A range of research opportunities is available, though the focus tends to be on encyclopedias stored on CD-ROM disks. The teachers follow a traditional mental model. In our experience, the schools and teachers who use technology in this way for instructional purposes tend to use it in limited ways for their own purposes as well. The critical point here is not just the approach to computers but the thinking behind the approach (the perceptual orientation), which limits the type of computer instruction.

At Instructional Approach 2

This approach expands the uses of technology, although such use continues to be within a fairly well-defined framework. Teachers use more projects in which material is embedded and emphasize the teaching of concepts as well as content. One of the most powerful changes is adding simulations, which range from simple expeditions with problems to solve to sophisticated complex scientific processes that can be monitored and mapped. We also find a richer use of multimedia.

Computers may be in labs, but the labs are likely to be more sophisticated with more flexible access. Classrooms also contain so-phisticated equipment and provide opportunities for students to work on their assignments at their own pace. One of the more interesting developments is using computers for authentic assessment. An example is the Grady Profile (1995). Student portfolios are created in multiple ways—ranging from documents to hypermedia stacks of performances on video.

At Instructional Approach 3

Technology is naturally embedded in the learning context and is often so smooth that no distinction is made between technology and the rest of the environment. Teachers move to an open space format focused on student-led projects. We have reported three examples of this rich integration in *Education on the Edge of Possibility* (Caine and Caine 1997):

• *In a Los Angeles magnet school* described in the *Los Angeles Times* (Blair and Konley 1995). Every desk has a computer, but you would be hard-pressed to find it. Computing is taught in the context of other subjects.

• *In the Creative Learning Plaza* (Caine and Caine 1997). Groups of up to 150 high school students work together in a high-tech environment, with facilitators rather than teachers. Each student is on the World Wide Web, and all work stations are on an intranet. The thrust of education is project based, with curriculum embedded in the projects.

• ***In the Space Islands Project*** (Johnson 1995). At one stage, this project was the largest educational program on the Internet. It linked students from hundreds of schools in many countries in a collective endeavor to design a space station using the old fuel tanks of the space shuttle.

In our experience, educators who facilitate these programs tend to be highly computer literate. They surf the Web, use computers for personal reasons, and embed technology in their daily and work lives.

In contexts of this type, teachers are working at a very sophisticated level. Their approach is formulated around active processing rather than on the construction of experiences for students. Students question their own conclusions; teachers challenge student thinking. Logical and scientific thinking is frequently joined with metaphoric thinking, poetry, music, and art. Computers are used on an as-needed basis to draw models, access information for projects, access experts in a field, do computations, and write.

How the Perceptual Orientations Drive the Use of Technology

Each dimension of the perceptual orientations plays itself out fairly clearly in the use of technology:

• ***From Power over Others to Self-Efficacy.*** Perhaps the most obvious difference among the perceptual orientations is the difference between downshifting and self-efficacy. Many educators are frightened of technology and feel helpless trying to use it. Their fear leads to circumscribing and fragmenting how they use computers. Perceptual Orientation 3 thinkers are more likely to feel free to experiment. In our experience, they also feel freer to allow students who are computer literate to take an active role in supporting other students and teaching the teacher.

• ***Expanded Cognitive Horizons.*** To embed technology in multiple ways, teachers must have expanded cognitive horizons, a Perceptual Orientation 3 characteristic. In part, this effort involves a grasp of a richer context in which technology is seen as related to everything else.

• *Self-Reference and Process.* Self-reference is critical in technologically rich and complex environments. For example, the Creative Learning Plaza depends upon facilitators' ability to process projects and experiences with students in real time, and to introduce complex ideas and curricular issues into discussions when appropriate. For teachers to genuinely and effectively assist students to reflect on and process their experience, they must be able to model such reflection.

• *From Control to Building Relationships That Facilitate Self-Organization.* A dynamic is necessary for projects to take on a life of their own. Students need opportunities to communicate with each other, search for information, pool resources, and work individually and collectively. Hence, for the projects to live, teacher MUST be able to let go of control and both facilitate and trust the project, the context, and the students to self-organize. Students should be able to use computers and technology as well as multiple other sources (e.g., real-world interviews, libraries, texts, rare books, membership in nature or community organizations, and historical artifacts).

Multiple Intelligences

We focus on a recent article (Gardner 1995) in which Howard Gardner discusses the uses and abuses of his theory on multiple intelligences. His theory originally postulated that there are at least seven different "intelligences," and that they are or could be active in any classroom. The seven intelligences are linguistic, logical-mathematical, musical, spatial, bodily-kinesthetic, intrapersonal, and interpersonal. He contends that traditional education and testing has largely focused on what he calls mathematical and linguistic intelligences.

Gardner shows that he is a Perceptual Orientation 3 thinker through the following comment:

> MI [multiple intelligences] theory is in no way an educational prescription. . . .

> Indeed, contrary to much that has been written, MI theory does not incorporate a "position" on tracking, gifted education, inter-disciplinary curricula, the layout of the school day, the length of

the school year, or many other "hot button" educational issues. I have tried to encourage certain "applied MI efforts," but in general my advice has echoed the traditional Chinese adage "Let a hundred flowers bloom" (Gardner 1995, p. 206).

What Gardner calls prescription is what we see as fundamental to Instructional Approach 1. We interpret his comments to mean that it was never his intent to have the theory of multiple intelligences limited to Instructional Approach 1, which tends to be highly prescriptive. Also, he clearly establishes that he has given his theory form but is allowing schools and educators to "self-organize" their interpretations and instruction, given his thinking and ideas based on research. This approach reflects the essence of Perceptual Orientation 3 thinking.

At issue is the type of thinking that leads to misusing the multiple-intelligences theory. In this particular article, he also mentions that several uses have "jarred" him. If we put those uses into the context of our model of instruction, the approaches that jar fit easily into a traditional Instructional Approach 1 format—one that is too narrow for and does not do justice to Gardner's complex theory.

At Instructional Approach 1

We give four examples of how we think Gardner's theory has been misinterpreted, using our theory of instruction as the framework:

• ***"The attempt to teach all concepts or subjects using all the intelligences"*** (Gardner 1995, p. 206). Here multiple intelligences is used as a delivery model in which teachers do not question the relationship between the intelligences and specific subjects. They take for granted that educators are to use the intelligences to teach a subject. This understanding of Gardner's theory suggests both narrow cognitive horizons and an unexamined acceptance of a Perceptual Orientation 1 system.

• ***"The belief that it suffices, in and of itself, just to go through the motions of exercising a certain intelligence"*** (Gardner 1995, p. 206). Here the teacher assumes that using an intelligence equates with good teaching. That assumption is incorrect. An Instructional Approach 1 application of any intelligence will still produce relatively trivial results.

- *"The use of intelligences primarily as mnemonic devices"* (Gardner 1995, p. 206). This example hints strongly of traditional teaching. Mnemonic devices are meant to facilitate memorization. A song, for instance, may connect parts of the body or the presidents of the United States. What we have here is the creative practice and rehearsal of surface knowledge—unquestionably Instructional Approach 1. Clearly there can be benefits because memorization at times is important. In our terms, however, this type of instruction has little to do with dynamical learning in new and living contexts.

- *"The direct evaluation (or even grading) of intelligences, without regard to context or content"* (Gardner 1995, p. 207). One can only guess at how teachers "grade" the intelligences. It strikes us that once again teachers who do this type of grading have a simplistic idea of how the intelligences work. Grading of intelligence suggests that a particular intelligence is somehow independent of context and other intelligences the learner has or is capable of developing. Grading of intelligences also suggests that teachers are reducing the theory to fit into Instructional Approach 1 guided by Perceptual Orientation 1 thinking.

In the preceding examples, the multiple-intelligences theory is construed to suit traditional teaching. We speculate that such teaching still fragments the entire learning process and that testing drives instruction. We also suspect that teachers who apply the multiple-intelligences theory with this approach still select what is to be done and learned.

Teachers at Instructional Approach 1 control teaching with direct instructional methods. These methods may include several of the intelligences by allowing children to draw their answers or design a song to memorize something. Gardner's theory is more likely to be interpreted as opportunities for colorful ways to deliver a lesson.

We acknowledge, however, that once teachers begin to explore the notion of multiple intelligences, they may find themselves rethinking what they are doing. Such reflection can lead to significant growth when accompanied by process groups, modeling, and intelligent feedback.

At Instructional Approach 2

This approach is where Gardner's theory can begin to flourish. Designed experiences, such as learning centers and teacher-orchestrated lessons, permit room for varying approaches and individual expression. Professionally packaged software programs include student activities that allow for individual differences. Students can begin to explore ideas and experiences from several perspectives. Indeed, such teaching provides natural possibilities for movement from Instructional Approach 2 to Instructional Approach 3.

Projects like making a videotape documenting an historical event, for example, could include students developing the sequence of the tape; inserting and creating supportive background music, artwork, and interviews with survivors; and writing an appropriate dialogue based on how the survivors might have felt, with technical assistance from computers and technology. Teachers acting as facilitators for such a project would have to be multitalented or have access to other experts. They would also inevitably learn from their students. If the experiences are complex enough, then students can explore and express their own unique intelligences and also begin to expand additional abilities.

At Instructional Approach 3

An excellent example of Instructional Approach 3 using the multiple intelligences occurs in one of Gardner's preferred models—the school as a museum. Here, children explore, conduct research, are challenged, work with all the intelligences in multiple and interactive ways, and experience the type of complex open space that demands facilitation rather than direct instruction. This approach is only possible when educators function at Perceptual Orientation 3, because they need to relinquish control, free up the context to allow for student experimentation, capitalize on student research, and see that rich curriculum can naturally emerge in its own time.

Whole Language

Perhaps nowhere in modern educational debate do the perceptual orientations manifest themselves more clearly than in the controversy over whole language. The debate has been carried on in newspapers, professional journals, professional meetings, and state departments of education. In California, this controversy has ended up in policies assuring that children will be taught phonics in a broad literacy program instead of being taught whole language (Colvin 1997).

As originally conceived, whole language involves what we call Instructional Approach 3. Ellis (1996), relying on the work of Goodman (1986) and Weaver (1990), summarizes whole language:

> What is whole language? Whole language is not a prescribed curriculum but a philosophy of teaching in which all the language arts are integrated in a meaningful context for each child. Whole language focuses on meeting individual needs in natural learning environments in which students learn to assume responsibility for their own learning. There is no one right approach; however, typically, most whole language programs will include daily writing time from self-selected topics, daily reading time from self-selected books, reading and writing sharing experiences, teacher read-alouds, teacher-modeled reading and writing, use of children's literature and writing across the curriculum, reading and writing conferences between peers and between teacher and student, and small-group cooperative work. Whole language engages children in language and literature throughout the school day. In whole language, strategies instead of skills are emphasized and are presented in meaningful contexts, and the teacher assumes the role of facilitator of learning rather than dispenser of information (p. 3).

While reading and language are embedded across the curriculum, students can make choices, and teachers can select a wide range of ordinary experiences to foster a mastery of language. Reading aloud, modeling writing, and using cooperative groups also help. Directed practice of specific skills occurs during daily writing time and in conferences with students.

At Instructional Approach 1

"Whole language at Instructional Approach 1" is an oxymoron, because whole language cannot be fragmented into parts as an instructional technology. To call traditional teaching whole language is like offering a crumb instead of the loaf. To a genuine whole language teacher, reducing the possibilities in whole language to teaching phonics or to simply reading aloud several times are foolishness. Both phonics and reading aloud are only part of the whole language repertoire. Such fragmentation and limited learner experience inhibits the acquisition of complex skills and mastery of language. For example, teachers may select good children's literature, but it may be "work-booked to death" (Ellis 1996, p. 4); or they may offer literature with no attention to the skills and processes embedded in it. The problem is that many teachers do not have the understanding that permits an expansion of their teaching:

> Many districts and states are mandating whole language, not understanding the philosophical base that is essential if teachers are going to implement it. Textbook publishers and commercial businesses are picking up the name of whole language to promote materials (Shannon 1992). Many whole language advocates are concerned that a whole language philosophy is in danger of being increasingly misunderstood and misapplied. There is also concern that this reform movement will be curtailed because practices . . . and instructional materials contrary to the philosophy are being promoted in the name of whole language (Weaver 1990) (Ellis 1996, p. 4).

Instructional Approach 1 is inappropriate for such a complex philosophy. The need to fragment the curriculum, make it fit into precise, quantifiable chunks, including time, ignores the "whole" in whole language. Examples we have seen are traditional teachers and district mandates that insist on students reading 12 instead of 9 books, and the use of rewards (such as pizzas) for reading focusing on quantity of books read.

At Instructional Approach 2

Parts of whole language can be implemented at Instructional Approach 2. Group activities can provide complex experiences even if they are teacher directed and highly organized. This type of learning is part of any whole language classroom. The problem is limiting language to practice and rehearsal or to technical and scholastic knowledge. What is missing is the flow and naturalness, where students and teachers share their respective enthusiasm for reading, learning, and each other's ideas.

At Instructional Approach 3

Whole language requires a complex world view and broad cognitive horizons—characteristics of teachers at Perceptual Orientation 3 using Instructional Approach 3. First, such teachers are competent in the field itself. Second, they can see the ways that language, reading, and writing penetrate and connect with all parts of the curriculum and with the many experiences that students have. Time restrictions are not a major concern because there is no need to push for the mastery of a specific aspect of a skill within time parameters. Rather, teachers grasp how learning develops and how opportunities and teachable moments can both be orchestrated and present themselves.

Instructional Approach 3 teachers have the self-confidence to know that they can orchestrate student experiences and capitalize on student interests and on the situation, so that the dictates of a prescribed curriculum and sequence of mandated steps can be augmented and incorporated, not followed step by step. Interactions between students and between adults and students use language naturally. These interactions occur when teachers let go of control and allow self-organization within the class. Students express their interests, select books, work with each other, and participate in projects. Critical thinking occurs in both students and teachers, with constant and deep reflection on what is transpiring and on how to improve the process.

Fun and Games—Understanding One Another

In a letter to the *Los Angeles Times* (Letter to the Editor, August 27, 1996), Ted Sizer is taken to task for suggesting that the curriculum be integrated in small ways by combining two subjects. The writer says that this suggestion is absurd because it would require a teacher to grade 180 essays on two different subjects, rather than just 90 essays on one subject. The writer further infers that a teacher would end up teaching in two different departments.

We see a classic clash of perceptions. The writer takes fragmentation of the curriculum, separation of departments, and grading of student papers for granted, and does not see the possibility of integrating different subject areas into something larger or more dynamic. Each perceptual orientation regards some things as totally obvious, and yet they differ profoundly on what these things are. Perhaps what frustrates everyone most is a collective inability of those with different perceptual orientations to communicate with each other.

Perceptual Orientation 1 and 2 thinkers can communicate with each other, but Perceptual Orientation 3 thinkers are just different. From a Perceptual Orientation 1 and much of a Perceptual Orientation 2 perspective, Perceptual Orientation 3 thinkers often cannot translate what they do from a Perceptual Orientation 1 or 2 perspective. They are heard as being vague and elusive or idealistic. They appear to be exclusive and not share how they get the results they get. Yet when Perceptual Orientation 3 thinkers get together even as strangers, they understand each other. We witnessed this connection when the Perceptual Orientation 3 teachers from Dry Creek and Park View met for the first time. They told us they "knew" each other as if they had been friends for years. They told us they knew who the others were just by looking around the room! Perceptual Orientation 3 thinkers recognize this almost uncanny intimacy they can have with strangers, even while they remain strangers to those with whom they work more closely. Teachers at the New Jersey Writing Project, a successful literacy and whole language teacher education program in Texas—which facilitates Perceptual Orientation 3 thinking—speak of the same uncanny linkages.

We saw this frustration with language firsthand when two successful Perceptual Orientation 3 thinkers were told to teach other teachers in the school how to do brain-based teaching. Everyone was frustrated because the Perceptual Orientation 1 and 2 thinkers were looking for strategies that worked, and the Perceptual Orientation 3 thinkers were deeply engaged in a flowing "whole" community in which skills and information were embedded naturally. At the same time, the quest for effective strategies is legitimate and important.

What we hope to accomplish is to shine some light on the nature of the clashes in perception and the approaches to instruction. With that goal in mind, we can clarify a developmental path for teachers and improve teacher education.

11

Developing Brain-Based Teachers

Individuals who can think in complex ways can help children access the potential with which they are endowed. Irrespective of where teacher education occurs, the bottom line is that the sophisticated instruction needed for the next century requires a major mind shift that goes beyond improved instructional strategies.

Ultimately, what we want to see is people who are at Perceptual Orientation 3 and who can use Instructional Approaches 1 through 3. When they are also grounded in a theory of learning such as ours, which draws from the neurosciences, they are what we call brain-based teachers. That combination is the one we most wish to encourage and develop. Perceptual Orientation 3 thinking incorporates the flexibility, intellectual breadth, ability to handle active uncertainty, and self-confidence that are critical to supporting learning organized around student purposes and meanings. We fervently believe that tomorrow's success stories will be written by those who can think, question, make decisions, utilize computers and the arts for creative explorations, perceive complex patterns, and make connections. There will be an enormous disparity between those who can function in complex ways in a fluid world and those who rely on rote-learned procedures that operate in an unchanging mechanistic world. For this reason, educators should be aiming much higher and further than mastery of the basics. Students whose educational experience never transcends the delivery model of teaching will tend not to master the more complex aspects of learning and will be left behind. As will their society.

We should add that being a Perceptual Orientation 3 thinker does not guarantee proficiency at Instructional Approach 3, but it is a prerequisite. From this enlarged perspective, an understanding of Instructional Approach 3 becomes possible. Then, training may help, though we have found that Instructional Approach 3 tends to emerge as people with the appropriate perceptual orientation look anew at themselves and their colleagues and begin to explore possibilities on their own.

Because the process is an inward-looking one in which personal change takes place and egos need to be dealt with, becoming a Perceptual Orientation 3 thinker is voluntary and largely self directed. It is impossible to create a Perceptual Orientation 3 thinker if that person doesn't want to become one. Looking inward is a prerequisite for individuals accurately assessing themselves. The teachers engaged in our process have little difficulty pinpointing where they are in their own teaching and thinking. Many have volunteered to say, "I am at Instructional Approach 1, moving into Instructional Approach 2, and I'm becoming a Perceptual Orientation 2 thinker."

The process is extremely difficult without time and support, particularly using process groups, which we advocate and used in our schools. We are also convinced that the entire change process requires additional coaching, preferably from someone outside the school. The environmental constraints within schools are too powerful for any one individual or group to begin to move too far beyond the status quo. Obviously, this kind of knowledge also requires district and community understanding and support.

The lack of time for reflection and thinking in almost all U.S. schools leaves little hope for a process of this type to work without changing systems priorities. As we mention in *Education on the Edge of Possibility* (Caine and Caine 1997), Japanese and Chinese elementary school teachers spend 40 percent of their time designing curriculum, discussing individual students, and preparing for their teaching. In the West, particularly in the United States, a delivery approach without adequate and ongoing reflection and deliberation almost ensures teaching that does not go beyond delivering knowledge in traditional ways. Particularly during this time of knowledge explosion in almost every field, when the need to understand and work with computers is vital, educators have no time in the day or any official plan for how they might move out of a traditional and outdated approach to teaching. Teachers, like all of us, need time and opportunities to rethink pedagogy, so that they can reflect on their own present assumptions and learn about alternatives.

Developmental Path

Our work has a developmental path, showing clear differences among the three perceptual orientations. As a teacher's perceptual orientation expands, the range of instructional approaches available increases. But this process is not linear.

Many teachers appear to be quite traditional—seeming to be at Perceptual Orientation 1 and using Instructional Approach 1—but we often found that the context dictated this type of teaching. As we document in our research, schools have many natural Perceptual Orientation 3 thinkers in search of a theory that justifies their world view. We suspect that the real data behind beginning teachers quitting the profession early is related to some of the more complex thinkers feeling constricted in these Perceptual Orientation 1 environments.

Different Types of Teachers

We find that integrating the instructional approaches and the perceptual orientations is useful:

• *Traditional Teachers—Perceptual Orientation 1/Instructional Approach 1.* This pattern describes teachers at Perceptual Orientation 1 who use Instructional Approach 1 exclusively. When we talk about traditional teachers, this combination is what we mean. The primary focus is on the acquisition of surface knowledge—that is, the transmission of facts to be memorized and skills to be rote learned.

• *Technical/Scholastic Teachers—Perceptual Orientation 2/Instructional Approaches 1 and 2.* This pattern begins with teachers at Perceptual Orientation 2. Because their world view is expanded, they are capable of functioning both at Instructional Approaches 1 and 2. Thus, they have the capacity to teach for memorization and for the acquisition of technical/scholastic knowledge. This type of teaching is most popular in Europe and Asia. It is also the focus of current U.S. reform. We discuss this topic in Chapter 4.

• *Wholistic/Constructivist/Brain-Based Teachers—Perceptual Orientation 3/Instructional Approaches 1, 2, and 3.* Constructivist teachers are individuals whose perceptual reality is grounded in the characteristics we identified as belonging to Perceptual Orientation 3. They are capable of mastering all three instructional approaches. This richer and more complex repertoire and functioning makes possible teaching for deep understanding, or what we call the construction of dynamical knowledge.

From our perspective, most public schools, private schools, and home schooling are based on traditional teaching—Perceptual Orientation 1 thinking and Instructional Approach 1. School districts and boards that guide these schools also adhere to this combination. Collectively, society's experiences and beliefs are grounded in Industrial Era approaches to teaching, which does not incorporate advanced research in teaching. The prevalence of this traditional frame of reference suggests that many of the systemic changes beginning to take place may only be cosmetic. For example, it is possible to raise grades and test scores when class sizes are reduced and parents are supportive, but the future demands a more complex approach to education.

Teacher Education—Foundational Issues

Universities have not been left untouched by the confusion permeating K–12 education. From our perspective, they, too, are caught between the differences in thinking and practice explored in this book.

In fact, the question of whether universities should "train" teachers at all is hotly debated, and already several universities have eliminated teacher education altogether. In California, training teachers is now open to school districts and other, viable professional organizations, many of whom claim to prepare teachers faster and with less paperwork for students. Some even promise a master's degree simultaneously with the credential. The state, in desperate need to get new teachers into the classroom as quickly as possible, is letting the marketplace determine the most expedient and efficient way to fill this need. There is talk of creating a potential tier system to deal with more advanced training for teachers at some future time—one a university might most appropriately provide.

Regardless of who is in charge of preparing teachers, most of the teacher preparation available today does not address the kinds of complex issues that we see looming on the horizon and that we outline here and in *Education on the Edge of Possibility* (Caine and Caine 1997). Today's teacher preparation inevitably builds on the thinking and practice dominated by the industrial model and factory metaphor (Instructional Approach 1 and Perceptual Orientation 1). Teachers within universities are still largely instructed in how to "deliver" content and skills to students, how to control student behavior using punishment and rewards, and how to grade students on the basis of work done. This kind of teaching becomes an inadequate foundation for the Information Age and for learning extended by technological possibilities. Even if teacher preparation programs include "modern" methods, such as cooperative learning or thematic instruction, the inclusion of such methods is often poorly understood and not subscribed to by all faculty. Confusion is exacerbated when faculty members subscribe to differences in philosophical and theoretical beliefs as critical foundations for practice.

From the perspective of our theory and experience, we make the following recommendations for a foundational program of teacher education. It assumes a four-year undergraduate degree that provides both broad and specific subject matter knowledge and incorporates (we hope) other experiences of teaching besides the deeply entrenched delivery model.

Primary Purpose

We suggest that teacher preparation should prepare Perceptual Orientation 3 thinkers. This preparation involves a transformational process that provides the foundation for all competencies and capacities. This change emphasizes the need for continuous process and process groups. We believe that cohort groups are essential. Additional learning should concentrate on the following six focuses.

Focus 1: Developing a Coherent Mental Model of Learning

Anyone planning to teach should understand how people learn, from infancy through adulthood, and such knowledge should become a mental model. Inadequate mental models and world views these future teachers hold should be challenged. A close look at learning should also include a thorough understanding of how they (future teachers) themselves learn. The problem that exists now is that future teachers are confronted with fragmented theories and content so broad that the information can only be memorized. Little time is available to make such information meaningful or challenge the deeply entrenched beliefs that guide how they plan to teach. In our words, what they learn can by definition be little more than surface knowledge. Many educational psychology texts, for example, which are often the only encounter with learning theory that students experience, include a superficial collection of every theory, technique, and research experiment that could potentially have implications for an understanding of learning. This approach to instruction is tantamount to handing students an encyclopedia and telling them to use it to write poetry. Such an educational psychology text remains helpful but more as a reference guide or encyclopedia of research and theories on learning and teaching.

The brain/mind principles or similar meta-analysis would serve as a more focused foundation, providing a clear connection between theory and educational practice. Although university faculty may be highly specialized in their own research, explorations on how human beings learn should be synthesized and organized around foundational issues such as memory, the search for meaning, the role of emotions in learning, the role of individual differences, and brain plasticity and development. We, of course, would recommend the brain/mind learning principles. This synthesis should also include and allow for continually updating and sharing information from current research in education, in multiple fields, and in the neurosciences; it should permeate assumptions underpinning all topic areas of focus.

Focus 2: Instruction—Mastering the Instructional Approaches

Closely tied to the use of technology is a thorough understanding of pedagogy. Again, in our terms, we would invite students to identify the various instructional approaches and experience the promise and limitations of each. How the instructional approaches interact with the use of technology would be of paramount significance. Mastering Instructional Approach 3 should be seen as critical to teaching in any technologically rich or complex environment.

Focus 3: Understanding Technology as a Way of Infusing Life and Meaning

The goal should be to naturally infuse technology into lives filled with meaning and purpose. All credentialed teachers should be thoroughly grounded in the use of computers and technology. Thus, technology should be tied to pedagogy, with the ultimate goal being mastery of all the instructional approaches, particularly mastery of Instructional Approach 3. Among the facets to incorporate are extensive grounding in available software and developmental trends; mastery of e-mail and Internet and Web searches; multimedia applications; and ways in which technology is infusing practical daily living.

Focus 4: Using Perceptual Orientation 3 Thinking as the Foundation for Helping Students Master Multiculturalism Within a Democratic Society

We see much confusion about individuality and diversity and how these are managed in a society based on democratic principles. Students should have the capacity to deal with individual differences and cultural, ethnic, and religious differences without compromising the whole of society. Perceptual Orientation 3 thinking, with its emphasis on interconnectedness and complexity, is a foundation for this capacity. A grasp of complexity and systems thinking, along with the implications of the new science and how to live it, naturally aids students in understanding how variations in an infinite variety can fit within a democratic and complex system. This kind of thinking and understanding should be the exit goal for every teacher.

Focus 5: Progressing from Discipline by Coercion to Creation of Collaborative Communities

Our research demonstrated that it is not possible to move from Instructional Approach 1 to 2 without changing the classroom climate to one of responsible collaboration. Students as well as teachers need superior communication skills, including common technical language, conflict resolution, a common organizational framework, inter- and intrapersonal means of communication, self-reflection, and self-understanding. Students of tomorrow need to learn from such teachers, and these teachers need to know how to create such environments and help students learn to communicate more effectively in all sorts of settings. Our experience suggests that a grasp of coherence, orderliness, and the dynamics of process groups is crucial. We describe these areas in detail in *Education on the Edge of Possibility* (Caine and Caine 1997) and illustrate our own process in *Mindshifts* (Caine, Caine, and Crowell 1994).

Focus 6: Curriculum—Functioning in a World That Makes Sense

Curriculum needs to be rethought. Although much has been done on defining the core curriculum, the integrated curriculum, and more, we are currently working with others in the quest for principles and processes that would shape a new paradigm curriculum. We frame our thinking on curriculum in terms of the parameters that define Perceptual Orientation 3 thinking, the characteristics of the possible human that we introduce in Chapter 2, and the principles of connectedness that conclude this book.

Practice

Our six focuses beg the question: Will students graduating from such programs teach in Perceptual Orientation 1 schools and systems and find themselves incompatible with the expectations and parameters expected of them? We know that some efforts to bring Perceptual Orientation 3 thinkers and complex environments such as the Creative Learning Plaza (see Caine and Caine 1997) into districts have been sabotaged by a system that requires teachers to teach linearly, using behavioral objectives for students and teaching for the test. Genuine, systemic change calls for partnerships between districts and universities, but such partnerships must deal with thinking and ideas based on a sound theory of learning as well as on a revised view of practice. Genuine partnership means combining problem solving with mutual respect for others' challenges and dilemmas. In effect, districts and universities need to offer inservice education to each other to provide the kind of continuity that has a new, coherent ground of learning and practice for new as well as seasoned teachers and educators.

We are beginning such an experiment this fall in the Yucaipa/Calimesa Joint Unified School District in southern California. The middle school we have been working with, particularly D-track, has served as a model within the district. Recently, the district established a new elementary school, and the vice principal from the middle school along with two top teachers from D-track will lead the school in a brain-based approach. Renate will continue to work with the two schools (supported by a grant from the district). She will work with other volunteers in process groups throughout the district. She will also become available to the high school should they choose to work with her. The entire process is for volunteers only, and no effort is made to force or impose brain-based learning on the community or the schools. Collaboration means people of like minds exploring common connections, and that is how this experiment is evolving. At the same time, Renate and her colleague Sam Crowell will be offering graduate courses in an experimental master's program designed to focus on a brain-based approach to learning and instruction. The program will be offered onsite in the district at the middle school.

Our hope is that ultimately a better understanding and a growing partnership in brain-based learning and teaching will develop and that such a partnership will provide continuity between the university foundational preparation and the opportunities for practice, student observation of modeling, and opportunities for future teachers to intern. Slowly and carefully, we will collectively attempt to weave a partnership that helps bridge a way out of the Industrial Era and metaphor into what it means to be educators and learners in the Information Age.

A Closing Word

After all the research, observations, and collaboration, the question still looms large: What does it mean for human beings to use more of their brains? We have suggested some characteristics of the possible human, but what do such human beings really look and act like? How do they think? How dependent are they on drugs and pharmaceuticals? On fiber optics and technology? What can they do with their brains and minds?

At present and in the coming years, we all will be dealing with immensely complicated questions. The concerns about cloning and our overall control over physical life are examples. Certainly questions concerning our environment are others. The mechanistic and reductionist paradigm has given us a science that seems to believe that it can do anything, so much so that many people have embarked on the path of creating "intelligent" machines and synthetic life.

And yet, do we really know what it is to be intelligent? Is a philosophy and way of living that discounts the mind, dismisses the soul, and consumes life itself really the greatest expression of human intelligence of which we can conceive?

Recently, a scientist working with cloning animals was asked if the moral implications bothered him. He responded by saying that ethics and moral implications were not his domain, and that he tended to leave such questions to others. This man has passed every test from 1st grade through his Ph.D. He has done complex research and is an expert in his field. By many standards he would be seen as intelligent. But is he?

According to most traditional definitions, there would be no doubt about it. But when we apply the notion of the interconnectedness of all life that individuals with broad cognitive horizons have, then he is missing at least one vital connection. Knowing and carrying responsibility for our work is something we teach every child in kindergarten. Surely it needs to apply in adulthood as well.

If we talk about using more of our brain, then we cannot continue to compartmentalize life or learning. We must think and act in broader terms. We now know that information, cognition, and critical thinking do not operate in some sort of abstract vacuum. Our feelings, emotions, and values are always engaged. And a higher-order use of our brains must include, as a minimum, an ability to let go of erroneous, deeply entrenched beliefs and cognitive commitments when we are faced with new evidence and possibilities. Surely the ability to genuinely change our minds is a core component of intelligence.

We would also argue that ethics and intelligence must be linked, if only because an intelligent person appreciates the interconnectedness of all and acts accordingly. Similarly, we suspect that the almost total distinction currently made between the individual and the community will have to be modified. In many respects, the brain is a social brain. And in many respects, intelligence is a function of the way we interact in context. One probable result is that an intelligent person will, in some ways, be a person who is a member of an intelligent community.

We have found much solace in the new sciences, with its picture of a universe that is chaotic, ever changing, and yet intrinsically orderly. In a real sense, creativity is all around us and in us. We are here to create. But it is up to us whether our creativity is selfish and fragmented from a larger moral and ethical fiber, or our creativity explores and commits to creating the highest that human beings can achieve. We believe that the latter is possible.

What do we give our children who move and exist in this age of turbulence? With everything around them continually changing, what can we give them to understand that despite all they see, the world and universe make sense?

It seems to us that a world that expresses wholeness and is a place where everything is in relationship ought to be understandable in terms of some basic principles or "laws." Our challenge is to discern and live in accordance with the emerging laws that permeate our lives and the subjects that we explore.

In the past few years, we have been seeking to understand what we call principles of connectedness. We have borrowed unashamedly in our search, and have now begun to embed these principles in our work. Each "brain" chapter of *Mindshifts* (Caine, Caine, and Crowell 1994), for instance, is prefaced by one of them. We offer them to you as the beginning of our understanding of a paradigm in which science is respected while life remains sacred. And where wholeness itself is natural:

Principles of Connectedness

The whole is greater than the sum of the parts.
Reality is both linear and nonlinear.
Inner and outer reflect each other.
Order is present everywhere.
Reality consists of matter, energy, and meaning.
Everything is both part and whole simultaneously.
What is, is always in process.
Everything comes in layers.
Stable systems resist change—dynamic systems exist by changing.
Everything is separate and connected.
Rhythms and cycles are present everywhere.
The whole is contained in every part.

Bibliography

Abbott, J. (1994). *Learning Makes Sense.* Hertfordshire, United Kingdom: Education 2000.

Abbott, J. (1995). Report given to Prime Minister Major's Policy Unit at 10 Downey Street.

Abraham, F.D., and A.R. Gilgen, eds. (1995). *Chaos Theory in Psychology.* Westport, Conn.: Praeger.

Agnati, L.F., B. Bjelke, and K. Fute. (July 1992). "Volume Transmission in the Brain." *American Scientist* 80: 362–373.

Aguayo, R. (1990). *Dr. Deming: The American Who Taught the Japanese About Quality.* New York: Simon and Schuster.

Alexander, C.N., and E.J. Langer, eds. (1990). *Higher State of Human Development.* New York: Oxford University Press.

Allen, P.M. (1993). *Nonlinear Dynamics and Evolutionary Economics,* edited by R.H. Day and P.E. Chen. New York: Oxford University Press.

Allman, W.F. (1994). *The Stone Age Present.* New York: Touchstone.

Amabile, T. (1983). *The Social Psychology of Creativity.* New York: Springer-Verlag.

Anderson, C.W., and E.L. Smith. (May 1985). "Teaching Science." In *The Educators' Handbook: A Research Perspective,* edited by V.E. Koehler. New York: Longman, Inc.

Apple, M.W.E., and J.A. Beane, eds. (1995). *Democratic Schools.* Alexandria, Va.: ASCD.

Armstrong, T. (1994). *Multiple Intelligences in the Classroom.* Alexandria, Va.: ASCD.

Aron, E., and A. Aron. (1986). *The Maharishi Effect: A Revolution Through Meditation.* Walpole, N.H.: Stillpoint Publishing.

Arthur, W.B. (1994). Keynote presentation at 4th Annual Chaos Network Conference, Denver, Colorado.

Ashton, P.T., and R.B. Webb. (1986). *Making a Difference: Teachers' Sense of Efficacy and Student Achievement.* New York: Longman, Inc.

Bandura, A. (April 20, 1992). "Self-Efficacy Mechanism in Sociocognitive Functioning." Audiotape of a presentation at the annual meeting of the American Educational Research Association, San Francisco.

Banks, S., and L. Renwick. (June 8, 1997). "Technology Remains Promise, Not Panacea." *Los Angeles Times*, p. A29.

Battistich, V., D. Solomon, M. Watson, and E. Schaps. (1994). "Students and Teachers in Caring Classroom and School Communities." Paper presented at the annual meeting of the American Educational Research Association, New Orleans.

Becker, E. (1968). *The Structure of Evil.* New York: The Free Press.

Begley, S. (February 19, 1996). "Your Child's Brain: How Kids Are Wired for Music, Math, and Emotions." *Newsweek*, pp. 57–61.

Benson, G.D., and W.J. Hunter. (December 1992). "Chaos Theory: No Strange Attractor in Teacher Education." *Action in Teacher Education* 14, 4: 61–67.

Blair, B.G., and R.N. Caine, eds. (1995). *Integrative Learning as the Pathway to Teaching Holism, Complexity, and Interconnectedness.* Lewiston, N.Y.: The Edwin Mellen Press.

Blair, J., and P. Konley. (April 22, 1995). "Something So Right at One Public School." *Los Angeles Times*, p. 87.

Boettcher, W.S., S.S. Hahn, and G.L. Shaw. (1994). "Mathematics and Music: A Search for Insight into Higher Brain Function." *Leonardo Music Journal* 4: 53–58.

Bohm, D. (November 6, 1989). "On Dialogue: Meeting of November 6, 1989" (booklet). Ojai, Calif.: David Bohm Seminars.

Bonstingl, J.J. (1992). *Schools of Quality: An Introduction to Total Quality Management in Education* (rev. ed. 1996). Alexandria, Va.: ASCD.

Bopp, J., M. Bobb, L. Brown, and P. Lane. (1984). *The Sacred Tree: Reflections on Native American Spirituality.* Lethbridge, Alberta, Canada: Four Worlds Development Press.

Bower, B. (1995). "Images of Intellect: Brain Scans May Colorize Intelligence." *Science News* 146: 236.

Boychuk, B. (December 22, 1995). "There's No Such Thing as a Free Federal Program." *Los Angeles Times*, p. B9.

Brauth, S.E., W.S. Hall, and R.J. Dooling, eds. (1991). *Plasticity of Development.* Cambridge, Mass.: The MIT Press.

Briggs, J.P., and F.D. Peat. (1985). *Looking Glass Universe: The Emerging Science of Wholeness.* Great Britain: Fontana Paperbacks.

Briggs, J., and F.D. Peat. (1989). *Turbulent Mirror: An Illustrated Guide to Chaos Theory and the Science of Wholeness.* New York: Harper and Row.

Brown, J.L., and E. Pollitt. (February 1996). "Malnutrition, Poverty, and Intellectual Development." *Scientific American* 274, 2: 38.

Caine, R.N., and G. Caine. (1991). *Making Connections: Teaching and the Human Brain.* Alexandria, Va.: ASCD.

Caine, R.N., and G. Caine. (1994a). *Making Connections: Teaching and the Human Brain* (rev. ed.). Menlo Park, Calif.: Addison-Wesley Publishing Company.

Caine, R.N., and G. Caine. (April 1994b). "Patterns of Wholeness: Can Complexity and Systems Theory Help Us Understand Restructuring of Schools?" Paper presented at the annual conference of the American Educational Research Association, New Orleans.

Caine, R.N., and G. Caine. (April 1995). "Reinventing Schools Through Brain-Based Learning." *Educational Leadership* 52, 7: 43.

Caine, R.N., and G. Caine. (1997). *Education on the Edge of Possibility.* Alexandria, Va.: ASCD.

Caine, G., R.N. Caine, and S. Crowell. (1994). *Mindshifts: A Brain-Based Process for Restructuring Schools and Renewing Education.* Tucson, Ariz.: Zephyr Press.

California State Board of Education. (1988). *California Social Science Framework.* Sacramento: California Department of Education.

Calvin, W.H., and G.A. Ojemann. (1994). *Conversations with Neil's Brain: The Neural Nature of Thought and Language.* Reading, Mass.: Addison-Wesley Publishing Company.

Campbell, S. (1995). "A Sense of the Whole: The Essence of Community." In *Community Building: Renewing Spirit and Learning in Business,* edited by K. Gozdz. San Francisco, Calif.: New Leaders Press.

Cannon, A. (February 4, 1996). "The Mood of America." *Austin American-Statesman,* pp. D1–D5.

Capra, F. (1988). *The Turning Point: Science, Society, and the Rising Culture.* New York: Simon and Schuster.

Capra, F. (February 1995). *From the Parts to the Whole: Systems Thinking in Ecology and Education.* The Professional Development Briefs: Fourth Annual Colloquium, Burlingame, Calif.: California Staff Development Council (CSDC).

Capra, F. (March 1995). "Creating Community Through Ecoliteracy: An Ecological Model for School Innovation and Reform." Paper presented at the annual conference of the Association for Supervision and Curriculum Development, San Francisco.

Capra, F. (1996). *The Web of Life.* New York: Anchor Books.

Carr, C. (1994). *The Competitive Power of Constant Creativity.* New York: American Management Association.

Casey, K. (1995). "The New Narrative Research in Education." In *Review of Research in Education*, edited by M.W. Apple. Washington, D.C.: American Educational Research Association.

Chalmers, D.J. (December 1995). "The Puzzle of Conscious Experience." *Scientific American* 273, 6: 80–86.

Chapman, G. (January 11, 1996). "'Friction-Free' Economy Rhetoric Holds a Time Bomb." *Los Angeles Times*, p. D2.

Chapman, G. (February 22, 1996). "'Jumping On—and Off—the Technology Bandwagon." *Los Angeles Times*, pp. D2–D5.

Churchland, P.S. (1986). *Neurophilosophy: Toward a Unified Science of the Mind/Brain*. Cambridge, Mass.: The MIT Press.

Cleveland, J., J. Neuroth, and S. Marshall. (November 1995). *Learning on the Edge of Chaos: Complex Adaptive Systems Theory and Human Learning, First Draft*. Lansing, Mich.: On Purpose Associates.

Clifford, P., and S.L. Friesen. (September 1993). "Teaching and Practice: A Curious Plan." *Harvard Educational Review* 63, 3: 339–358.

Cochran-Smith, M., and S.L. Lytle. (March 1990). "Research on Teaching and Teacher Research: The Issues That Divide." *Educational Researcher* 19, 2: 2–9.

Collier, G. (1973). *Inside Jazz*. London: Quartet Books.

Colborn, T., D. Dumanoski, and P. Peterson Myers. (1996). *Our Stolen Future*. New York: The Penguin Group.

Colvin, R.L. (May 5, 1995). "Teachers Speak Out in Favor of Reading Aloud." *Los Angeles Times*, p. 3.

Colvin, R.L. (December 8, 1995). "Eastin's School Reform Plan Scaled Back." *Los Angeles Times*, pp. A1–A40.

Colvin, R.L. (May 20, 1997). "Board Members Fear Lag in Phonics Instruction." *Los Angeles Times,* p. B3.

Combs, A.W. (1991). *The Schools We Need: New Assumptions for Educational Reform*. Lanham, Md.: University Press of America.

Combs, A.W., R. Blume, A. Newman, and H. Wass. (1974). *The Professional Education of Teachers*. 2nd ed. Boston: Allyn and Bacon.

Combs, A.W., A.C. Richards, and F. Richards. (1988). *Perceptual Psychology*. Lanham, Md.: University Press of America.

Combs, A.W., and D. Snygg. (1959). *Individual Behavior. A Perceptual Approach to Behavior*. New York: Harper and Row.

Crowell, S. (1989). "A New Way of Thinking: The Challenge of the Future." *Educational Leadership* 47, 1: 60.

Crowell, S., G. Caine, and R.N. Caine. (1997). *The Reenchantment of Learning*. Tucson, Ariz.: Zephyr Press.

Csikszentmihalyi, M. (1990). *Flow: The Psychology of Optimal Experience.* New York: Harper Perennial.

Csikszentmihalyi, M. (1993). *The Evolving Self: A Psychology for the Third Millennium.* New York: HarperCollins.

Curwin, R.L., and A.N. Mendler. (1988). *Discipline with Dignity.* Alexandria, Va.: ASCD.

Damasio, A.R. (1994). *Descartes' Error: Emotion, Reason, and the Human Brain.* New York: Avon Books.

Darling, D.J. (1996). *Zen Physics: The Sense of Death, the Logic of Reincarnation.* New York: HarperCollins.

Darling-Hammond, L.E., ed. (1994). *Review of Research in Education.* Washington, D.C.: American Educational Research Association.

Day, R.H., and P.E. Chen. (1993). *Nonlinear Dynamics and Evolutionary Economics.* New York: Oxford University Press.

DeAngelis, T. (September 1995). "A Nation of Hermits: The Loss of Community." *The APA Monitor* 26, 9: 1.

De Bono, E. (1970). *Lateral Thinking.* New York: Harper and Row.

DeChardin, P.T. (1976). *The Heart of Matter.* New York: Harcourt Brace Jovanovich.

Deci, E.L., R.E. Driver, L. Hotchkiss, R.J. Robbins, and I.M Wilson. (1993). "The Relation of Mothers' Controlling Vocalizations to Children's Intrinsic Motivation." *Journal of Experimental Child Psychology* 55, 2: 151–162.

Deci, E.L., and R.M. Ryan. (1987). "The Support of Autonomy and the Control of Behavior." *Journal of Personality and Social Psychology* 53, 6: 1024–1037.

Deci, E.L., A.J. Schwartz, L. Sheinman, and R.M. Ryan. (1981). "An Instrument to Assess Adults' Orientations Toward Control Versus Autonomy with Children: Reflections on Intrinsic Motivation and Perceived Competence." *Journal of Educational Psychology* 73, 5: 642–650.

Deci, E.L., W.H. Spiegel, R.M. Ryan, R. Koestner, and M. Kauffman. (1982). "Effects of Performance Standards on Teaching Styles: Behavior of Controlling Teachers." *Journal of Educational Psychology* 74, 6: 852–859.

Del Prete, T. (1990). *Thomas Merton and the Education of the Whole Person.* Birmingham, Ala.: Religious Education Press.

Dennett, D.C. (1991). *Consciousness Explained.* Boston: Little, Brown and Company.

Dewey, J. (1938). *Experience and Education.* New York: Collier Books.

Dewey, J. (1944). *Democracy and Education.* New York: The Free Press.

Dewey, J. (1962). *Reconstruction in Philosophy.* Boston: The Beacon Press.

Diamond, M.C. (1988). *Enriching Heredity: The Impact of the Environment on the Anatomy of the Brain.* New York: The Free Press.

Dienstbier, R.A. (January 1989). "Arousal and Physiological Toughness: Implications for Mental and Physical Health." *Psychological Review* 96, 1:
84–100.

Dolan, W.P. (1994). *Restructuring Our Schools: A Primer on Systemic Change.*
Kansas City: Systems and Organizations.

Dole, J.A., and G.M. Sinatra. (April 1994). "Beliefs and Conceptual Change:
Research in Social and Cognitive Psychology." Paper presented at the
annual meeting of the American Educational Research Association, New
Orleans.

Doll, W.F. (1993). "A Post-Modern Perspective on Curriculum." *Advances in
Contemporary Educational Thought.* New York, Teachers College, Co-
lumbia University.

Doll, W.E. (1995). "Ghosts and the American Curriculum: Search for a Neo-
pragmatic Cosmology." Unpublished paper for Eidos Institute, St. Peters-
burg, Russia.

Driscoll, M.E. (April 1994). "School Community and Teacher's Work in Urban
Settings: Identifying Challenges to Community in the School Organization." Paper presented at the annual meeting of the American Educational
Research Association, New Orleans. (Available from New York University).

Dryfoos, J.G. (1994). *Full-Service Schools: A Revolution in Health and Social
Services for Children, Youth, and Families.* San Francisco: Jossey-Bass.

Duffy, T.M., and D.H. Jonassen, eds. (1992). *Constructivism and the Technology
of Instruction: A Conversation.* Hillsdale, N.J.: Lawrence Erlbaum.

Eccles, J.C. (1989). *Evolution of the Brain: Creation of the Self.* London:
Routledge.

Eccles, J.C. (1994). *How the Self Controls Its Brain.* Berlin: Springer-Verlag.

Edelman, G.M. (1992). *Bright Air, Brilliant Fire: On the Matter of the Mind.* New
York: Basic Books.

Egan, K. (1989). *Teaching as Story Telling: An Alternative Approach to Teaching
and Curriculum in the Elementary School.* Chicago: University of Chicago Press.

Egol, M. (1994). *Information Age Accounting: Catalyst and Enabler of the
Self-Organizing Enterprise.* New York: Arthur Anderson.

Eisler, R. (1987). *The Chalice and the Blade.* San Francisco: Harper and Row.

Ekman, P., and R.J. Davidson, eds. (1994). *The Nature of Emotion: Fundamental
Questions.* New York: Oxford University Press.

Elbow, P. (1986). *Embracing Contraries: Explorations in Learning and Teaching.* New York: Oxford University Press.

Ellis, N. (1996). "Collaborative Interaction as Support for Teacher Change."
Paper presented at the annual meeting of the American Educational
Research Association, San Francisco.

Elmore, R.F. (December 1995). "Structural Reform and Educational Practice." *Educational Researcher* 24, 9: 23–26.

Fadiman, D. (1988). *Why Do These Kids Love School?* (videotape). Menlo Park, Calif.: Concentric Media.

Fellmeth, R.C. (July 5, 1995). "California: A Society That Cuts Child Welfare But Boosts Jails." *Los Angeles Times*, p. B7.

Fernlund, P.M. (1995). "Teaching for Conceptual Change." In *Integrative Learning as the Pathway to Teaching Holism, Complexity, and Interconnectedness*, edited by B.G. Blair and R.N. Caine. Lewiston, N.Y.: The Edwin Mellen Press.

Fiske, E.B. (1992). *Smart Schools, Smart Kids: Why Do Some Schools Work?* New York: Simon and Schuster.

Flanigan, J. (January 10, 1996). "With Its New Lab, Caltech Has a Formula to Survive Uncertainty." *Los Angeles Times*, pp. D1–D11.

Flores, B., P.T. Cousin, and E. Diaz. (1991). "Transforming Deficit Myths About Language, Literacy, and Culture." *Language Arts* 68, 5: 369–379.

Flores, B.E., E. Garcia, S. Gonzales, G. Hidalgo, K. Kaczmarek, and T. Romero. (1986). *Holistic Bilingual Instructional Strategies*. Phoenix, Ariz.: Exito.

Fogarty, R.E., ed. (1993). *Integrating the Curricula: A Collection*. Palatine, Ill.: IRI/Skylight Publishing, Inc.

Francis, D. (1995). *Wild Horses*. New York: Jove Books.

Freeman, W.J. (1995a). "The Kiss of Chaos and the Sleeping Beauty of Psychology." In *Chaos Theory in Psychology*, edited by F.D. Abraham and A.R. Gilgen. Westport, Conn.: Praeger.

Freeman, W.J. (1995b). *Societies of Brains: A Study in the Neuroscience of Love and Hate*. Hillsdale, N.J.: Lawrence Erlbaum.

Fullan, M.G., and S. Stiegelbauer. (1991). *The New Meaning of Educational Change*. New York: Teachers College Press.

Gablik, S. (1991). *The Reenchantment of Art*. London: Thames and Hudson.

Gardner, H. (1985). *Frames of Mind: The Theory of Multiple Intelligences* (rev. ed. 1993). New York: Basic Books.

Gardner, H. (1991). *The Unschooled Mind: How Children Think and How Schools Should Teach*. New York: Basic Books.

Gardner, H. (1993). *Multiple Intelligences: The Theory in Practice*. New York: Basic Books.

Gardner, H. (November 1995). "Reflections on Multiple Intelligences." *Phi Delta Kappan* 77, 3: 200–208.

Garmston, R., and B. Wellman. (April 1995). "Adaptive Schools in a Quantum Universe." *Educational Leadership* 52, 7: 6.

Gates, W.H. (1995). *The Road Ahead*. New York: Viking.

Gateva, E. (1991). *Creating Wholeness Through Art.* Aylesbury, Bucks, United Kingdom: Accelerated Learning Systems, Ltd.

Gazzaniga, M. (1985). *The Social Brain: Discovering the Networks of the Mind.* New York: Basic Books.

Gazzaniga, M. (1992). *Nature's Mind: The Biological Roots of Thinking, Emotions, Sexuality, Language, and Intelligence.* New York: Basic Books.

Gell-Man, M. (1994). *The Quark and the Jaguar.* New York: W.H. Freeman and Company.

Gendlin, E.T. (1962). *Experiencing and the Creation of Meaning.* Glencoe, Calif.: The Free Press of Glencoe.

Gendlin, E.T. (1981). *Focusing.* 2nd ed. New York: Bantam Books.

Gerard, G., and L. Teurfs. (1995a). *The Art and Practice of Dialogue* (audiotape series). California: The Dialogue Group.

Gerard, G., and L. Teurfs. (1995b). "Dialogue and the Learning Organization." Paper presented at Session M20 of the National Conference of the American Society for Training and Development, Dallas.

Gilovich, T. (1991). *How We Know What Isn't So: The Fallibility of Human Reason in Everyday Life.* New York: The Free Press.

Glatthorn, A.A. (1994). *Developing a Quality Curriculum.* Alexandria, Va.: ASCD.

Goerner, S.J. (1994). *Chaos and the Evolving Ecological Universe.* Langhorne, Pa.: Gordon and Breach Science Publishers.

Goerner, S.J. (1995). "Chaos and Deep Ecology." In *Chaos Theory in Psychology,* edited by F.D. Abraham and A.R. Gilgen. Westport, Conn.: Praeger.

Goguen, J.A., and R.K. Forman, eds. (1994). "Journal of Consciousness: Controversies in Science and the Humanities." *An International Multi-Disciplinary Journal,* Vol. 1, UK and USA: Imprint Academic.

Goleman, D. (1995). *Emotional Intelligence: Why It Can Matter More Than IQ.* New York: Bantam Books.

Goodlad, J.I. (1984). *A Place Called School: Prospects for the Future.* San Francisco: McGraw-Hill.

Goodlad, J.I. (1990). *Teachers for Our Nation's Schools.* San Francisco: Jossey-Bass.

Goodlad, J.I., R. Soder, and K.A. Sirotnik, eds. (1990). *The Moral Dimensions of Teaching.* San Francisco: Jossey-Bass.

Goodman, K. (1986). *What's Whole in Whole Language?* Portsmouth, N.H.: Heinemann.

Goodman, K., and Y. Goodman. (1979). "Learning to Read Is Natural." In *Theory and Practice of Early Reading,* edited by L. Resnick and P. Weaver. Hillsdale, N.J.: Lawrence Erlbaum.

Gozdz, K., ed. (1995). *Community Building: Renewing Spirit and Learning in Business.* San Francisco: New Leaders Press.

Grady Profile [computer software]. (1995). St. Louis, Mo.: Aurbacher Associates, Inc.

Gruneberg, M.M., and P.E. Morris. (1979). *Applied Problems in Memory.* London: Academic Press.

Hanh, T.N. (1976). *The Miracle of Mindfulness!: A Manual on Meditation.* Boston: The Beacon Press.

Harman, W. (1988). *Global Mind Change: The Promise of the Last Years of the Twentieth Century.* Indianapolis: Knowledge Systems, Inc.

Harman, W. (September 1992). "The Shifting World View: Toward a More Holistic Science." *Holistic Education Review* 5, 3: 16–17.

Harste, J.C. (1989). *New Policy Guidelines for Reading: Connecting Research and Practice.* Urbana, Ill.: National Council of Teachers of English and the ERIC Clearinghouse on Reading and Communication Skills.

Hart, L. (1983). *Human Brain, Human Learning.* New York: Basic Books.

Herrnstein, R.J., and C. Murray. (1994). *The Bell Curve: Intelligence and Class Structure in American Life.* New York: The Free Press.

History-Social Science Curriculum Framework and Criteria Committee. (1987). *History-Social Science Framework.* Sacramento: California State Department of Education.

Hobson, J.A. (1994). *The Chemistry of Conscious States: How the Brain Changes Its Mind.* Boston: Little, Brown and Company.

Hooper, J., and D. Teresi. (1986). *The 3-Pound Universe.* New York: Dell Publishing Company.

Houston, J. (1982). *The Possible Human: A Course in Enhancing Your Physical, Mental, and Creative Abilities.* Los Angeles: J.P. Tarcher, Inc.

Houston, R.W. (1986). *Mirrors of Excellence: Reflections for Teacher Education from Training Programs in Ten Corporations and Agencies.* Reston, Va.: Association of Teacher Educators.

Hyman, R., and B. Rosoff. (1984). "Matching Learning and Teaching Styles: The Jug and What's In It." *Theory into Practice* 23, 1: 35–43.

Isaacs, W.N. (1993). "Taking Flight: Dialogue, Collective Thinking, and Organizational Learning." *Organization Systems* 22: 24–39.

It's Elementary. (1992). Elementary Grades Task Force Report. Sacramento, Calif.: California Department of Education.

Jacobs, H.H., and L. Nadel. (1985). "Stress-Induced Recovery of Fears and Phobias." *Psychological Review* 92, 4: 512–531.

Jaworski, J. (1996). *Synchronicity: The Inner Path of Leadership.* San Francisco: Berrett-Koehler.

Johnson, P.H. (November 22, 1995). "High School Students Mount Global Bid to Design Space Shuttle Pit Stop." *Los Angeles Times*, p. 4.

Jones, B.F., A.S. Palinscsar, D.S. Ogle, and E.G. Carr, eds. (1987). *Strategic Teaching and Learning: Cognitive Instruction in the Content Areas.* Alexandria, Va.: ASCD.

Journal of Consciousness Studies. Thorverton, United Kingdom: Imprint Academic.

Kaplan, P. (April 8, 1996). "School's Out—CD ROM's In." *Los Angeles Times*, p. D9.

Kauffman, D.L. (1980). *Systems 1: An Introduction to Systems Thinking.* Minneapolis, Minn.: S.A. Carlton.

Kauffman, S.A. (August 1991). "Antichaos and Adaptation." *Scientific American* 265, 2: 78–84.

Kauffman, S. (1995). *At Home in the Universe: The Search for the Laws of Self-Organization and Complexity.* New York: Oxford University Press.

Keidel, R.W. (1995). *Seeing Organizational Patterns.* San Francisco: Berrett-Koehler.

Kelso, J.A. (1995). *Dynamic Patterns: The Self-Organization of Brain and Behaviour.* Cambridge, Mass.: The MIT Press.

Kierstead, F., J. Bowman, and C. Dede, eds. (1979). *Education Futures: Sourcebook 1. Selections from the First Conference of the Education Section World Future Society.* Washington, D.C.: World Future Society.

Koehler, V., ed. (1985). *The Educator's Handbook: A Research Perspective.* New York: Longman, Inc.

Kofman, F., and P.M. Senge. (1993). "Communities of Commitment: The Heart of Learning Organizations." *American Management Association*, pp. 5–20.

Kohlberg, L. (1981). *The Philosophy of Moral Development.* New York: Harper and Row.

Kohn, A. (1990). *The Brighter Side of Human Nature: Altruism and Empathy in Everyday Life.* New York: Basic Books.

Kohn, A. (1993). *Punished by Rewards: The Trouble with Gold Stars, Incentive Plans, A's, Praise, and Other Bribes.* New York: Houghton Mifflin.

Kotulak, R. (April 11, 1993). "Research Unraveling Mysteries of the Brain: Unlocking the Mind." *Chicago Tribune*, p. 1.

Kotulak, R. (1996). *Inside the Brain: Revolutionary Discoveries of How the Mind Works.* Kansas City, Mo.: Andrews and McMeel.

Kuhl, P. (1994). "Learning and Representation in Speech and Language." *Current Opinion in Neurobiology* 4: 612–822.

Lakoff, G., and M. Johnson. (1980). *Metaphors We Live By.* Chicago: University of Chicago Press.

Langer, E. (1989). *Mindfulness*. Reading, Mass: Addison-Wesley Publishing Company.

Lawrence Hall of Science. (1992). *Full Option Science System (FOSS)*. Berkeley, Calif.: Encyclopedia Britannica Education Corporation.

Lazarus, R.S. (1991). *Emotion and Adaptation*. New York: Oxford University Press.

Leadership and the New Science (videotape). (1993). Script by K. McCarey. (Based on *Leadership and the New Science: Learning About Organization from an Orderly Universe*, by M.J. Wheatley, 1992). Carlsbad, Calif.: CRM Films.

LeDoux, J.E. (June 1994). "Emotion, Memory and the Brain." *Scientific American* 270, 6: 50–57.

Legge, J. (1990). *Chaos Theory and Business Planning: How Great Effects Come from Small Causes*. Melbourne, U.C., Australia: Schwartz and Wilkinson.

Letter to the Editor. (June 7, 1996). *USA Today*, p. 3A.

Letter to the Editor. (August 27, 1996). *Los Angeles Times*, p. E3.

Lieb, B., ed. (March 1993). "Achieving World Class Standards: The Challenge for Educating Teachers." *Proceedings of the OERI Study Group on Educating Teachers for World Class Standards*. Washington, D.C.: U.S. Department of Education.

Little, J.W. (1982). "Norms of Teacher Collegiality and Experimentation: Workplace Conditions of School Success." *American Educational Research Journal* 19: 325–340.

Lozanov, G. (1978a). *Suggestology and Outlines of Suggestopedy*. New York: Gordon and Breach Science Publishers, Inc.

Lozanov, G. (1978b). *Suggestology and Suggestopedy—Theory and Practice*. Working document for the Expert Working Group, United Nations Educational, Scientific, and Cultural Organization (UNESCO) Vol. ED-78/WS/119.

Macionnis, J.J. (1994). *Sociology*. 4th ed. Englewood Cliffs, N.J.: Prentice-Hall.

MacLean, P.D. (1978). "A Mind of Three Minds: Educating the Triune Brain." In *Education and the Brain*, edited by J. Chall and A. Mirsky. Chicago: University of Chicago Press.

Mainzer, K. (1994). *Thinking in Complexity: The Complex Dynamics of Matter, Mind, and Mankind*. New York: Springer-Verlag.

Mandela, N. (1994). *Inaugural Speech*. Republic of South Africa. Online source: http://www.sas.upenn.edu/African_Studies/Articles_Gen/Inaugural_Speech_17984.html.

Marshall, S.P. (January 1995). "The Vision, Meaning, and Language of Educational Transformation." *The School Administrator*, pp. 8–15.

Martin, S. (October 1994). "Music Lessons Enhance Spatial Reasoning Skills." *The APA Monitor* 26, 9: 5.

Martinez, J.L., and R.P. Kesner, eds. (1991). *Learning and Memory: A Biological View.* San Diego, Calif.: Academic Press.

Marzano, R.J. (1992). *A Different Kind of Classroom: Teaching with Dimensions of Learning.* Alexandria, Va.: ASCD.

Marzano, R.J., D. Pickering, and J. McTighe. (1993). *Assessing Student Outcomes: Performance Assessment Using the Dimensions of Learning Model.* Alexandria, Va.: ASCD.

Maslow, A.H. (1968). *Toward a Psychology of Being.* 2nd ed. New York: D. Van Nostrand Company.

McClure, R., ed. (February 1993). *Learning and Thinking Styles: Classroom Interaction.* Washington, D.C.: National Education Society.

McLaughlin, C., and G. Davidson. (1994). *Spiritual Politics: Changing the World from the Inside Out.* New York: Ballantine Books.

Meadows, D. (June 1982). "Whole Earth Models and Systems." *Co-Evolution Quarterly,* pp. 98–108.

Michaels, M. (1994). *Seven Fundamentals of Complexity.* Savoy, Ill.: People Technologies, The Chaos Network.

Miller, J.P. (March 1992). "Toward a Spiritual Curriculum." *Holistic Education Review* 5, 1: 43.

Miller, J.P. (1993). "Worldviews, Educational Orientations, and Holistic Education." In *The Renewal of Meaning in Education,* edited by R. Miller. Brandon, Vt.: Holistic Education Press.

Miller, N.E. (November 1995). "Clinical-Experimental Interactions in the Development of Neuroscience." *American Psychologist* 50, 11: 901–911.

Miller, R. (1990). *What Are Schools for? Holistic Education in American Culture.* Brandon, Vt.: Holistic Education Press.

Miller, R., ed. (1991). *New Directions in Education: Selections from Holistic Education Review.* Brandon, Vt.: Holistic Education Press.

Morley, D. (February 1993). "Chasing Chaos in Santa Fe." *Manufacturing Systems,* p. 40.

Morley, D. (October 1995). "Nonlinear Social Behavior." *Manufacturing Systems,* p. 16.

Morris, L. (1995). *Managing the Evolving Corporation.* New York: Van Nostrand Reinhold.

Moyers, B. (1993). *Healing and the Mind.* New York: Doubleday.

Nadel, L., and J. Wilmer. (1980). "Context and Conditioning: A Place for Space." *Physiological Psychology* 8: 218–228.

Nadel, L., J. Wilmer, and E.M. Kurz. (1984). "Cognitive Maps and Environmental Context." In *Context and Learning,* edited by P. Balsam and A. Tomi. Hillsdale, N.J.: Lawrence Erlbaum.

National Center for Education Statistics. (1995). *The Pocket Condition of Education 1995*. Washington, D.C.: U.S. Department of Education.

Neihardt, J.G. (1961). *Black Elk Speaks: Being. The Life Story of a Holy Man of the Oglala Sioux*. Lincoln: University of Nebraska Press.

Nerburn, K., and L. Mengelkoch, eds. (1991). *Native American Wisdom*. San Rafael, Calif.: The Classic Wisdom Collection, New World Library.

Nesmith, M. (August 1, 1996). *Los Angeles Times,* p. A5.

Neville, B. (1989). *Education Psyche: Emotion, Imagination, and the Unconscious in Learning*. North Blackburn, Victoria, Australia: Collins Dove.

Newell, A. (1990). *Unified Theories of Cognition*. Cambridge, Mass.: Harvard University Press.

Nieto, S. (December 1994). "Lessons from Students on Creating a Chance to Dream." *Harvard Educational Review* 64, 4: 392–426.

O'Keefe, J., and L. Nadel. (1978). *The Hippocampus as a Cognitive Map*. Oxford: Clarendon Press.

Oliver, D.W., and K.W. Gershman. (1989). *Education, Modernity, and Fractured Meaning: Toward a Process Theory of Teaching and Learning*. Albany: State University of New York Press.

Olsen, L. (1994). *The Unfinished Journey: Restructuring Schools in a Diverse Society*. San Francisco, Calif.: California Tomorrow.

Ornstein, R. (1991). *The Evolution of Consciousness: The Origins of the Way We Think*. New York: Prentice-Hall.

Pace, G., ed. (1994). "Whole Learning in the Middle School." In *A Learning Journey: Exploring Teaching and Learning in the Middle School Language Arts Classroom*, edited by P.T. Cousin and E. Aragon. Boston: Christopher Gordon Publishers.

Pascale, R.T. (1990). *Managing on the Edge: How the Smartest Companies Use Conflict to Stay Ahead*. New York: Simon and Schuster.

Patterson, J.L. (1993). *Leadership for Tomorrow's Schools*. Alexandria, Va.: ASCD.

Pelletier, K.R. (1994). *Sound Mind, Sound Body: A New Model for Lifelong Health*. New York: Simon and Schuster.

Penrose, R. (1989). *The Emperor's New Mind*. New York: Oxford University Press.

Penrose, R. (1994). *Shadows of the Mind: A Search for the Missing Science of Consciousness*. New York: Oxford University Press.

Perelman, L.J. (1992). *School's Out*. New York: Avon Books.

Perkins, D. (1992). *Smart Schools: From Training Memories to Educating Minds*. New York: The Free Press.

Perkins, D. (1995). *Outsmarting IQ: The Emerging Science of Learnable Intelligence*. New York: The Free Press.

Perrone, V.E., ed. (1991). *Expanding Student Assessment.* Alexandria, Va: ASCD.

Peters, R. (1985). "Notes on the Educational Imagination." (Unpublished review of Eisner, E.W., 1985, *The Educational Imagination—On the Design and Evaluation of School Programs.* 2nd ed. New York: Macmillan Publishing Company). California State University, San Bernandino.

Peterson, C., S. Maier, and M.E.P. Seligman. (1993). *Learned Helplessness: A Theory for the Age of Personal Control.* New York: Oxford University Press.

Phares, J.E. (1976). *Locus of Control in Personality.* Morristown, N.J.: General Learning Press.

Portfolio Submission Guidelines: Student Work Samples. (1995). Park View Middle School. Yucaipa, Calif.

Posner, G.J. (1989). *Field Experience Methods of Reflective Teaching.* White Plains, N.Y.: Longman, Inc.

Posner, G.J. (May 1992). "What Is Reflective Thinking and Why Is It Desirable?" Paper presented at the annual conference of the Association for Supervision and Curriculum Development, New Orleans.

Prigogine, I., and I. Stengers. (1984). *Order Out of Chaos: Man's New Dialogue with Nature.* New York: Bantam Books.

Purkey, W.W. (1970). *Self-Concept and School Achievement.* Englewood Cliffs, N.J.: Prentice-Hall.

Rauscher, F.H., G.L. Shaw, and K.N. Ky. (October 1993). "Music and Spatial Task Performance." *Nature* 365: 611.

Rauscher, F.H., G.L. Shaw, L.J. Levine, K.N. Ky, and E.L. Wright. (1995). "Listening to Mozart Enhances Spatial-Temporal Reasoning: Toward a Neurophysiological Basis." *Neuroscience Letters* 185: 44–47.

Richards, A.C., and A.W. Combs. (1992). "Education and the Humanistic Challenge." *The Humanistic Psychologist* 20, 2 and 3: 372–388.

Robertson, R., and A. Combs, eds. (1995). *Chaos Theory in Psychology and the Life Sciences.* Mahwah, N.J.: Lawrence Erlbaum.

Roehler, L.R., G.G. Duffy, M. Conley, B.A. Herrman, J. Johnson, and S. Michelsen. (April 1987). "Exploring Preservice Teachers' Knowledge Structures." Annual conference of the American Educational Research Association, Washington, D.C.

Rogers, C. (1969). *Freedom to Learn.* Columbus, Ohio: Charles E. Merrill Publishing Company.

Rose, S. (1993). *The Making of Memory.* New York: Anchor Books.

Rosen, R. (June 11, 1995). "In the '90's, Prisons Come Before Schools." *Los Angeles Times,* p. M5.

Roth, K.J. (April 1985). "Conceptual Change Learning and Student Processing of Science Texts." Paper presented at the meeting of the American Educational Research Association, Chicago.

Rottier, L. (October 1995). "If Kids Ruled the World: ICONS." *Educational Leadership* 53, 2: 51–53.

Routman, R. (1991). *Invitation:Changing as Teachers and Learners.* Portsmouth, N.H.: Heinemann.

Russell, P. (1979). *The Brain Book.* New York: Penguin Books.

Russell, P. (1995). *The Global Brain Awakens: Our Next Evolutionary Leap.* Palo Alto, Calif: Global Brain, Inc.

Samples, B. (December 1995). "Education as Love." *Holistic Education Review* 8, 4: 4–10.

Sarason, S.B. (1990). *The Predictable Failure of Educational Reform: Can We Change Course Before It's Too Late?* San Francisco: Jossey-Bass.

Sarason, S.B. (1993a). *The Case for Change: Rethinking the Preparation of Educators.* San Francisco: Jossey-Bass.

Sarason, S.B. (1993b). *Letters to a SERIOUS Education President.* Newbury Park, Calif: Corwin Press, Inc.

Scardamalia, M., and C. Bereiter. (1992). "Text-Based and Knowledge-Based Questioning by Children." *Cognition and Instruction* 9, 3: 177–199.

Scheffler, I. (1991). *In Praise of the Cognitive Emotions.* New York: Routledge.

Schein, E.H. (1993). "On Dialogue, Culture, and Organizational Learning." *Organizational Systems* 22, 2: 40–65.

Schon, D.A. (1983). *The Reflective Practitioner.* New York: Basic Books.

Schon, D.A. (1987). *Educating the Reflective Practitioner.* San Francisco: Jossey-Bass.

Schwartz, R. (March 1987). "Our Multiple Selves: Applying Systems Thinking to the Inner Family." *Networker*, pp. 25–83.

Schwartz, R. (November 1988). "When We Are Two: Know Thy Selves." *Networker*, pp. 21–29.

Selye, H. (1978). *The Stress of Life* (rev. ed.). New York: McGraw-Hill.

Senge, P.M. (1990). *The Fifth Discipline: The Art and Practice of the Learning Organization.* New York: Doubleday Currency.

Senge, P.M. (1996). *Introduction to Synchronicity: The Inner Path of Leadership.* San Francisco: Berrett-Koehler.

Shannon, P. (1992). *Becoming Political: Readings and Writings in the Politics of Literacy Education.* Portsmouth, N.H.: Heinemann.

Shapiro, S.B., and J. Reiff. (1993). "A Framework for Reflective Inquiry on Practice: Beyond Intuition and Experience." *Psychological Reports* 73: 1379–1394.

Sheldrake, R. (1988). *The Presence of the Past. Morphic Resonance and the Habits of Nature.* New York: Times Books.

Sleek, S. (December 1995). "Rallying the Troops Inside Our Bodies." *The APA Monitor* 26, 12: 1.

Spears, L.C. (1995). *Reflections on Leadership*. New York: John Wiley and Sons, Inc.

Spielberger, C.D., ed. (1972). *Anxiety: Current Trends in Theory and Research*, Vols. 1 and 2. New York: Academic Press.

Stacey, R.D. (1992). *Managing the Unknowable: Strategic Boundaries Between Order and Chaos in Organizations*. San Francisco: Jossey-Bass.

Stacy, D. (May 1994). "Cosmic Conspiracy: Six Decades of Government UFO Cover-Ups, Part Two." *Omni* 16, 8: 54–87.

Stedman, L.C. (April 1997). "International Achievement Differences: An Assessment of a New Perspective." *Educational Researcher* 26, 3: 4–15.

Sternberg, R.J. (1988). *The Triarchic Mind: A New Theory of Human Intelligence*. New York: Viking.

Stevenson, H.W. (December 1992). "Learning from Asian Schools." *Scientific American* 267, 6: 70–76.

Sylwester, R. (1995). *A Celebration of Neurons: An Educator's Guide to the Human Brain*. Alexandria, Va.: ASCD.

Taylor, W.C. (Reviewer). (November 1994). "Control in an Age of Chaos." *Harvard Business Review* 72, 6: 64–76.

Terry, N. (March 1992). "Where Learning Is the Adventure." *Zip Line* 21: 17–19.

Times Wire Service. (January 2, 1996). "Report Links Gene Variation to Novelty-Seeking Trait." *Los Angeles Times*, p. A13.

Vail, P.B. (1989). *Management as a Performing Art*. San Francisco: Jossey-Bass.

Vela, K. (February 1, 1996). *Letter: The Kids from Outerspace*. Dry Creek Elementary School: Rio Linda, Calif.

Vollmer, J. Local Control Project. (February 1996). P.O. Box 1535, Fairfield, Iowa, 52556.

Vygotsky, L.S. (1978). *Mind in Society*. Cambridge, Mass.: Harvard University Press.

Waldrop, M.M. (1992). *Complexity: The Emerging Science at the Edge of Order and Chaos*. New York: Simon and Schuster.

Wallace, B., and L.E. Fischer. (1987). *Consciousness and Behavior*. Newton, Mass.: Allyn and Bacon.

Wallace, R.K. (1993). *The Physiology of Consciousness*. Fairfield, Iowa: Institute of Science, Technology, and Public Policy and Maharishi International University Press.

Weaver, C. (1990). *Understanding Whole Language: From Principles to Practice*. Portsmouth, N.H.: Heinemann.

Webster's New World Dictionary of the American Language. (1960). Cleveland: The World Publishing Company.

Wheatley, M.J. (1992). *Leadership and the New Science: Learning About Organization from an Orderly Universe.* San Francisco: Berrett-Koehler.

Wheatley, M.J. (September 1995). "Leadership and the New Science." Presentation transcribed as Professional Development Brief No. 3. California State Development Council (CSDC).

Wheatley, M., and F. Capra. (September 1995). "A Diagogue." *The Professional Development Briefs: Fourth Annual Colloquium.* Burlingame, Calif.: California Staff Development Council (CSDC).

Wheatley, M.J., and M. Kellner-Rogers. (1996). *A Simpler Way.* Berrett-Koehler: San Francisco.

Whitehair, J. (December 1994). "Schools on the Move." *It's Elementary* 3, 18: 5.

Wilber, K. (1995). *Sex, Ecology, Spirituality: The Spirit of Evolution.* Boston: Shambhala Publications, Inc.

Wilson, D.L. (May 1995). "Seeking the Neural Correlate of Consciousness." *American Scientist* 83: 269–270.

Wood, G.H. (1992). *Schools That Work: America's Most Innovative Public Education Programs.* New York: Penguin Group.

Woolfolk, A.E. (1995). *Educational Psychology.* 6th ed. Needham Heights, Mass.: Allyn and Bacon.

World Book Dictionary. (1979). Reston, Va.: World Book.

Index

Page numbers in boldface refer to pages that contain figures.

About the Authors

Renate Nummela Caine is a professor of education at California State University, San Bernardino. She was an award-winning teacher and has worked at every level of education, from kindergarten to university. She consults on learning, teaching, and education throughout the United States and in other countries.

Geoffrey Caine is a learning consultant. He has taught in the fields of education, law, and management in universities in Australia and the United States. He has extensive experience in business and training, and consults throughout the United States and in other countries.

The Caines are also codirectors of Gossamer Ridge International, an organization that sponsors annual institutes that bring together leading edge thinkers to discuss issues in education. For more information, see http://www.gossamerridge.com

Renate and Geoffrey Caine can be reached at Caine Learning, P.O. Box 1847, Idyllwild, CA 92549 USA. See below for more information:

Telephone: 909-659-0152
Fax: 909-659-0242
E-mail: RNCaine@Wiley.CSUSB.edu
E-mail: gr@pe.net
Home page: http://www.cainelearning.com